BISHOP HARRY L. SEAWRIGHT

Publisher's Name: Bishop Harry L. Seawright

ISBN: 978-1-968442-10-1
Ebook: 978-1-968442-11-8

TABLE OF CONTENTS

FOREWORD

To the Reader

Some journeys are not measured by distance, but by devotion. Some callings are not announced loudly, but revealed through consistency, prayer, and obedience. *The Purple Robe* is not merely a book—it is a testimony bound in ink, a lived witness of what it means to walk faithfully through adversity and still emerge clothed in purpose. This work invites the reader into a life shaped by prayer long before recognition, by perseverance long before affirmation, and by faith long before reward. It tells the story of a man who did not begin with ease, access, or excess, but with resolve.

Raised in an era where opportunity was often denied and dignity was challenged, he learned early that survival required more than strength—it required vision, humility, and trust in God. Financial hardship, social barriers, and the weight of generational patterns were not just obstacles; they were assignments meant to be confronted and broken. At the heart of this book is a man of prayer. Not prayer as performance, but prayer as posture. Prayer as foundation. Prayer as breath. Time and again, the pages reveal how communion with God became both refuge and direction—how answers were received not through haste, but through waiting; not through self-reliance, but through surrender. This is the story of someone who learned how to seek help without shame, to receive instruction without pride, and to recognize that God's plan often unfolds through community, counsel, and obedience.

The Purple Robe is also the story of a builder. A builder of people, faith, vision, and institutions. With an uncompromising work ethic rooted in integrity, the author demonstrates what it means to labor not just for success, but for significance. He understands that excellence honors God and that diligence is a form of worship. The sacrifices, the long nights, the unseen labor—these are not footnotes in his journey; they are pillars of it. Throughout these pages, we encounter a man deeply connected to others. Friendship, mentorship, and wise counsel are not accessories to his calling; they are evidence of it. His humility allowed him to learn from all seasons of life, and his wisdom positioned him to pour into others with discernment and grace. Leadership, as shown here, is not dominance—it is service. Not elevation—it is responsibility.

This book does not shy away from setbacks. It names the obstacles. It honors the lessons learned through hardship, disappointment, and delay. Yet what stands out most is not the difficulty of the journey, but the faithfulness through it. Again and again, God's hand is evident—organizing, orchestrating, and confirming purpose in ways that could only be described as miraculous. At pivotal moments, divine confirmation arrived through unexpected voices, undeniable timing, and unshakable peace. A profound truth is revealed in these chapters: sometimes God accelerates what others assume must take decades. By the age of thirty-eight, accomplishments were reached that many do not experience until much later or not at all. These were not accidents. They were the result of obedience meeting opportunity and preparation meeting promise. The author's life stands as a testimony that when God calls, God equips, affirms, and sustains.

One of the most intimate gifts of this book is its structure. Through daily journaling and affirmations, readers are not merely observing a life—they are invited to walk in it, to process, reflect, and grow and examine their own faith, discipline, and calling. This book is an invitation to transformation, not inspiration alone.

Most importantly, *The Purple Robe* reveals what it truly means to wear purple—not as status, but as stewardship. Purple is not granted lightly. It represents sacrifice, responsibility, and spiritual investment. It signifies service to God's people, commitment to the Church, and the weight of leadership carried with reverence. This book teaches that purple is not worn for recognition, but for responsibility. Not for power, but for purpose.

What the reader will find here is not perfection, but faithfulness. Not self-promotion, but servanthood. Not a polished narrative, but an honest one. It is a life poured out—transparent, courageous, and anchored in Christ.

Only at the end of this foreword do I share this: I had the privilege of walking closely with this man for much of my life. In recent years, that closeness has deepened in ways that have shaped me profoundly. To witness this journey firsthand, to see the prayers, discipline, humility, and unwavering commitment to God has been life changing. I am immeasurably proud. It is with great honor that I recommend this book to you—not only as a reader, but as a grandson. And it is one of the greatest blessings of my life to say that this testimony, *The Purple Robe*, belongs to my grandfather, Bishop Harry L. Seawright.

May these pages strengthen your faith, challenge your walk, and remind you that God is still in the business of miracles.

Cameron I. Seawright

INTRODUCTION

Life is a journey, and my life has been a wonderful journey from my mother's womb to this day. I, like every one of you reading this book, have been the recipient of God's amazing grace. God has been with me every step of the way and I want Him to get all the glory He deserves.

Life can also be compared to a puzzle with many pieces. When put together properly, the pieces create a wonderful, beautiful, and powerful picture that emerges and brings joy to the Creator throughout eternity. God will continue to connect the pieces of your life. If we let Him He can and will put the pieces of everyone's life puzzle together in the right way.

He did this for me! He is still doing His work of connecting the dots in and for me. He is continuing to lead, guide, and show me the way. I just love it when the Holy Spirit speaks saying, *"This is the way; walk you in it."*

When I wrote the book, *Don't Faint: Help for Hurting Pastors and Their Families* I was excited about helping this group of individuals: hurting pastors and their families. I was a recovering hurting pastor with a myriad of experiences that had the potential of assisting other pastors to get through the maze of pastoring and family life. II Corinthians 1:3 – 5 compelled me to reach out to others:

> *"Blessed be God, even the Father of our Lord Jesus, the Christ, the Father of mercies, and God of all comfort; who comforts us in all our tribulation, that we may be able to comfort them which are in any trouble, by the comfort wherewith we ourselves are comforted of God."*

And now, God has called me again for I am compelled to write again. I am commanded and commissioned to enlarge my borders, expand my boundaries, and go into all the world. The message is for everyone everywhere: every gender, every home, every workplace, and every career. Why? Because God is no respecter of persons!

"He is not willing that all should perish, but that all should come to repentance." (II Peter 3:9).

So, I am eager to tell another part of my story. I want to give more of the *truth* that can and will motivate and set others free. The Harry L. Seawright story is intended to show that God is able. He is able to do, *"Exceeding, abundantly above all that we (anybody) can ask or think according to the power that works in us."*

God took me, the son of poor sharecropper parents from the little town of Swansea, South Carolina, and brought me from nowhere to somewhere; from being a nobody (in many people's eyes) to being somebody; from being uneducated, as some people would say, to a well-educated Christian, family man, and businessman extraordinaire who, in the summer of 2016, was blessed to be elected and consecrated as the 133rd Bishop in the African Methodist Episcopal (AME) Church, during the (AME) Church's 200th Year at the 50th Quadrennial General Conference in the city of Philadelphia, Pennsylvania.

If you allow, God can and will also do amazing things for you as you engage in your life's journey. God will do in you, for you, and through you, what only He can do. It will be your personal story just give God the glory!

CHAPTER ONE

The SOVEREIGN GOD IS IN CONTROL

I say, emphatically, that the omnipotent, omnipresent, omniscient, eternal, Jehovah, Elohim God is in total control. He was, is, and forever shall oversee the affairs of this world and humanity.

The title of this book, *The Purple Robe,* is a story of the truth that validates who is really in charge of all. This story will give God the glory for making something out of nothing. He stooped real low into a poverty-stricken family in Swansea, South Carolina, to show and tell that He is able.

It is essential that every reader who takes this journey with me proceeds with wisdom. However, to preserve this basic truth that God is in charge in all your going and getting, let understanding be primary and foundational. This is a story about the man, his ups, downs, struggles, victories, and triumphs. The bottom line is that this book is about the God of the man, and not simply about the man of God. Let us proceed to build this story. The scriptures have stood the test of time, including the criticisms of the simple, the neutral, and the sophisticated. The poor and the wealthy have turned to the scriptures and found integrity, reliability, power, and light for life, death, and beyond.

The Bible is the most sold book in all the history of humankind. Therefore, we will use the scriptures as our launching pad to confirm the truth of *The Purple Robe.* Although the word *'all'* is a small, monosyllabic word, it covers everything. Contextually, 'all' includes anything and everything and, excludes nothing. In II Timothy 3:16 the Word of God confirms,

"All scripture is given by inspiration of God and is profitable for doctrine, for reproof, for correction, for instruction in righteousness: that the man of God may be perfect, thoroughly furnished unto all good works. So that all scriptures are the Words of God."

A compelling and comforting sense of satisfaction comes with preserving the basic truth that God is in charge. It sets the captive and the victim free to see all God wants them to see. It causes them to believe that they can become all God intends them to be.

The Word of God gives the blessed assurance that we can go in confidence and do and be all that God has destined for us. The following texts from the holy scriptures provide a great foundation for us to establish ourselves, Hebrews 4:12 says,

"For the Word of God is quick, and powerful, and sharper than any two-edged sword, piercing even to the dividing asunder of soul and spirit, and of joints and marrow, and is a discerner of the thoughts and intents of the heart."

Numbers 23:19 says,

"God is not a man that He should lie; neither the son of man, that he should repent: has He said, and shall He not do it? Or has He spoken, and shall He not make it good?"

The scriptures identify Jesus of Nazareth, the virgin-born son, and child of Mary, as God in the flesh. Here is what the Scripture says in Matthew 1:21 – 23:

"And she shall bring forth a son, and you shall call His name Jesus: for He shall save His people from their sins. Now all this was done, that it might be fulfilled which was spoken by the prophet, saying, Behold, a virgin shall be with child, and shall bring forth a son, and they shall call His name EMMANUEL, which being interpreted is, God with us."

This reinforces that Jesus is God! Hallelujah! John 1, in verses 1, 2, 3, and 14, confirms the identity of Jesus.

"In the beginning was the Word, and the Word was with God, and the Word was God. The same was in the beginning with God. All things were made by Him, and without Him was not anything made that was made. And the Word was made flesh, and He dwelt among us, (and we beheld His glory the glory as of the only begotten of the Father), full of grace and truth."

Now it is no surprise why Jesus spoke with clarity and authority when He said to one of His disciples, Phillip, who implored of Jesus, *"Show us the way."* Jesus responded immediately saying, *"I am the way, the truth, and the life. No man comes to the Father but by Me," (John 14:6).*

Jesus doesn't stop with a little proclamation. He gives a confirmation to solidify the fact that He is 100% God, and 100% Man. He says,

"Heaven and earth shall pass away, but my words shall not pass away." (Mark 13:31).

Jesus also says, *"Think not that I am come to destroy the law and the prophets, but to fulfill them. For verily I say unto you, till heaven and earth pass, one jot nor one tittle shall not pass from the law till all be fulfilled." (Matthew 5:17-18).*

The Word of God brings hope to the hopeless. It brings light into darkness. It creates significance where there is low self-esteem and replaces the lack of drive to win with great success. It puts a burning fire in the desire to be the best one can be, despite a bad, awful, or slow start. Indeed, the Word of God will work for anyone, and everyone who believes. The following seven texts will always help, if tried and applied:

Number 1: "I can do all things through Christ, who strengthens me." (Philippians 4:13)

Number 2: "Call upon Me in your day of trouble. I will deliver you. And you shall glorify Me." (Psalm 50:15)

Number 3: "Be careful for nothing; but in everything by prayer and supplication with thanksgiving let your requests be made known unto God. And the peace of God, which passes all understanding, shall keep your hearts and minds through Christ Jesus." (Philippians 4:6-7)

Number 4: "In all your ways acknowledge Him and He (God) shall direct your path. Trust in the Lord with all your heart and lean not to your own understanding. Be not wise in your own eyes, but fear God and depart from evil." (Proverbs 3:5-7)

Number 5: "Have faith in God. For verily I say unto you, that whosoever shall say to this mountain, be thou removed, and be thou cast into the sea: and shall not doubt in his heart, but shall believe that those things which he says shall come to pass, he shall have whatsoever he says. Therefore, I (Jesus) say unto you, what things so ever you desire, when you pray, believe that you receive them, and you shall have them." (Mark 11:22-24)

Number 6: "And this is the confidence that we have in Him (Jesus), that if we ask (The Father), anything according to His will, He hears us: whatsoever, we ask, we know we have the petitions we desired of him." (1 John 5:14-15)

Number 7: "And I say unto you, ask, and it shall be given you; seek, and you shall find; knock, and it shall be opened unto you. For everyone that asks receives; and he that seeks, finds, and to him, that knocks it shall be opened. If a son shall ask bread of any of you that is a father, will he give him a stone? Or if he asks a fish, will he fish for a serpent? Or if he shall ask an egg, will he offer him a scorpion? If you then, being evil, know how to give good gifts to your children: how much more shall your heavenly Father give the Holy Spirit to them that ask Him?" (Luke 11:9-13)

Jesus makes it simple and plain for everyone! The seventh scripture listed above is sufficient to make a solid case that the Sovereign God is always in control. He is in charge; however, He has chosen to give mankind the opportunity to *taste and see* that the Lord is good, gracious, merciful, loving, kind, and forgiving. He wants every individual to discover what He has to offer by trial and error: testing, failing, and falling. Then, God blesses us through rising, again and again, even seven times, until victory is attained.

Our God is in total control, even when things appear to be totally out of control. He is the hope when everything seems hopeless. He is simply looking for someone, anyone who will believe His report, as Abraham did in Genesis 12:1-4.

God is still looking for anyone who will worship Him, in Spirit and in truth. He wants someone to love Him with all his/her heart, soul, mind, and strength. He, according to James 4:6 and 10, has a big surprise for anyone who will stand on His Word, the Holy Scriptures. "But He gives more grace."

Wherefore He says,

"God resists the proud but gives grace to the humble. Submit yourself to God. Resist the devil and he will flee from you. Draw nigh to God, and He will draw to you. Cleanse your hands, ye sinners, and purify your hearts, ye double minded. . . Humble yourselves in the sight of the Lord, and HE shall lift you up!" (James 4:6b -8,10)

Wherever you are, whoever you are, whatever is happening, has happened, or will happen, remain convinced that the Sovereign God will lift you up. He did it for me! He will do it for you! He is the Sovereign God. He is in charge! God is in control of everything that affects your present and future. Follow my story and join me in giving God glory.

CHAPTER TWO

A Slow Start by Faith

The holy scriptures are replete with multiple stories to demonstrate that God operates in a systematic way. We can learn an enormous amount of information about God and grow closer to know Him intimately by studying His works and His ways.

When I was chosen for the purple robe by God, I became the man, God's man, for a purpose. I had not done anything to deserve or earn this honor. God had already made this decision even before my parents met and before I was born. Therefore, the best way for me to magnify the Lord is to tell you about my parents first. God makes it clear in scripture from the creation of Adam that His plan for humankind includes everybody. It is because of this that we know and understand that all humanity came from the creation of one man and woman, Adam and Eve.

There are many examples that testify to the fact that parents play a vital role in helping produce the chosen person. When childbearing seemed impossible, Abraham and Sarah bore a child in their old age; however, scripture reminds us that nothing is impossible with God.

Isaac was miraculously born. Isaac grew up, to meet Rebecca and out of their union, Jacob was born. Jacob and his wife Rachel gave birth to Joseph. Jessie, the son of Obed, and his wife gave birth to a son named David. David and Bathsheba connected to give the world Solomon. Years later, the Holy Ghost moved mysteriously upon Mary, the virgin girl, to give the world Jesus.

"God moves in a mysterious way. His wonders to perform. He plants His footsteps in the sea and rides upon the storm. God's purposes are ripening fast and unfolding every hour. The bud may have a bitter taste, but sweet will be the flower." ("Light Shining out of Darkness" by William Cowper, translated into a hymn by John Newton).

In keeping with this same story, God caused my parents to connect and marry, and out of their union came eight children. I was the youngest. Because my daddy had serious health issues, in God's infinite wisdom, He knew that the odds were against our family. God had a plan to take a most unlikely child from poverty and see him through a public-school education, a single parent rearing, the shame of illegal alcohol sales, and college and university training to build a successful family and pastoral shepherding to become the 133rd elected and consecrated bishop in the AME Church.

In retrospect, my life, from my father's death when I was only 5 years old, could be called a slow start. My family and I were, however, stung and stunned by Daddy's absence. Daddy's death hit me hard, but since I was not old enough to fully understand the future implications and complications that would result because of his death, I didn't worry and stress.

The family's only plans were to carry on and make the most out of a bad situation. So, we took life one day at a time. Everybody understood that each person had to do their part individually to ensure our collective survival as a family.

The lowly Seawright family of sharecroppers did what sharecroppers do. We started working in the fields picking cotton and beans, while seasonally gathering corn and other vegetables.

With no father to lead us or work, we found ourselves with a problem that would eventually lead to an eviction. The reason was simple: the land had to be farmed, and we were not able to produce. Things now had gone from bad to worse. We were forced off the property and compelled to leave a house that my parents lived in for 20 years.

I categorize this as a slow start. My family began with the weight of poverty, racism, the loss of a father, and living with my mother who only had a ninth-grade education, and no insurance policy or inheritance. My mother, my siblings and I would learn for ourselves that,

> *"The eye of the Lord runs to and fro throughout the whole earth to show Himself, strong on behalf of those whose hearts are perfect toward Him,"* (II Chronicles 16:9).

The only reason we survived the struggle is that God was with us. He provided for us. Emmanuel! He protected us. He literally made a way out of no way. So, we could not see the end from the beginning. But God did! He even saw every step along the way.

One of the most interesting things about my family's story is we did not know where we were going or what we were doing. In a span of eight years, we moved to five different houses. These houses had no indoor bathrooms or running water. They were dilapidated buildings that had holes in the walls, broken windows, and leaky roofs. But thanks be to God, we kept on living, moving, and improving by taking one day at a time!

My mother was young, but she was strong. She had a super work ethic which made a positive difference for us. I inherited the spirit of hard work from her. There was not any honest work that was too lowly or humiliating for my mother to do for the purpose of providing for her family. I saw this with my own eyes, and it motivated me!

My real motivation came when my mother's toils, troubles, defeats, and triumphs ultimately ended with us moving into a home. This was a milestone I'll never forget. By working, saving money, being patient, exercising faith, eventually she did what seemed to be the impossible. She purchased an acre of land and borrowed money to build a two-bedroom house.

This was our house, The Seawright's house and we were pleased. We were proud of the fact that we had our own place to call home, but when we moved in, we knew we could and would stay in this house. My three brothers and I would have to share one room. My mother had her own bedroom. My sister and her daughter slept in the living room.

At this point I simply did not know where I was going. I only knew that I was going along with life. Nothing dramatic or traumatic happened. Whatever was going on in my life at the time gave me opportunities. These opportunities allowed me to grow and know the truth about life. One truth that stood out to me was the truth about help. Help seemed to always be there for me. For instance, being the youngest child gave me the chance to be blessed with several opportunities my older siblings did not receive.

One opportunity was that I spent each summer in West Columbia, South Carolina. I lived with my sister, Louise, and her husband, David (Junior); I babysat their three children. Because this family was solid, I looked, listened, and learned from them.

I experienced first-hand what a good nuclear family should be, how they should act, and what they should say. My brother-in-law was a good, hard working father who cherished his family. My sister was hard working and smart, like our mother. She wanted only the best for their family. They modeled for the community what a real family looked and felt like.

It was at that moment that I caught the vision, and I made my decision about living. They had great family values. I chose to adopt those same values and emulate what I learned and loved. While my start in life was slow, it was a good start, and I was taking it one day at a time. After making this decision, however, I decided to shift from low gear to the next gear with a little stretching of the facts about my age. My mother was reluctant, but she allowed me to elevate my age on a job application. I was determined to find employment beyond the vegetable fields.

Therefore, I entered the real workforce. I landed my first summer job at age 14 with The South Carolina State Mental Hospital. This was a facility for the mentally ill, not necessarily a fitting place for a first job at 14 years old. In spite of my deception God helped me. He also helped me leave the job after I was bullied, threatened, and intimidated by a guy much larger and a little older. Nevertheless, I was helped, again!

My oldest sister's husband, John Lee loaded trucks for a nearby transportation company. He was a stable force in my life. He taught me many things about manhood and how to take care of a family. He even taught me how to tie a necktie. I'll never forget John Lee, my brother-in-law, who helped me get a job as a truck loader. I worked that job after school, summers, and even while I was in college.

I continued to grow in my work ethic, which was profitable when work was slow at the trucking company. I worked as a short order cook, dishwasher, french fry cutter, cleaning technician, and a mail handler with the United States Postal Service. While I was still in high school, I also drove a school bus.

Life was now moving faster, and I was thinking I wanted to do something to improve myself. My sister, Louise, told me, *"When you work and make your own money, you can buy what you want."* I took her advice and so, I bought my first car at age 16. At age 18, I purchased a brand-new car, a 1974 Chevrolet Nova. I'll never forget the feeling!

As slow as things were going, the time clock kept ticking and graduation preparation was in full swing. I knew I wanted to go to trade school. I did not think highly of my high school grades, and my Scholastic Aptitude Test (SAT) scores were low. I decided that I would pursue plumbing as a trade. I also scored high on an electronics inventory test and was pursued by Bell and Howell Electronics School in Atlanta, Georgia. Furthermore, I wanted to work, have my own money, and help my mother.

Then, help came again. This time, in the person of Dianna Ginyard, one of my classmates. She suggested that I check out Benedict College where she was planning to attend. She was clear about the great opportunity for financial aid for Black American students through the state and federal government. We still stay in touch with each other. Today, Dianna is an anointed and powerful sister-in-Christ.

I did not know that the gears of my life were about to shift, but it did, to my wonderful surprise. I followed Dianna's idea and checked out Benedict College. I was accepted and received enough assistance to cover my tuition, and the Basic Educational Opportunity Grant (BEOG) covered my room and board. I was totally shocked and elated.

I knew of others who had succeeded in college. I had cousins who attended and graduated from college successfully. I had friends who had participated in the federally funded Upward Bound program. This program prepared students for the rigors of the college courses and the challenges that often come with college life. However, no one in my immediate family had gone to college. I would be the first among my siblings.

Certain so-called friends made fun of me and reminded me that Benedict College graduates could not find jobs. As I shut out the negative comments, God sent positive words for me through my mother, my sister, and a few people from my church. The encouragement enabled me to fight off the naysayers, the negative prognosticators, and the other blind guides. I felt free! I had a vision! I wanted to be better and do better. This was my chance.

CHAPTER THREE

CHOSEN, but Not Called

The scriptures are full of great stories of people who were chosen by God but were not called until a precise moment in time. God always has a plan that includes the best for humanity. God is love and because He is love, He will not force His will on His creation. He gives us free will. He gives us time and opportunities to accept His plan, purposes, and power. That is the way it is. The following people were chosen long before they were called: Noah, Abraham, Isaac, Jacob, Moses, Samuel, King Saul, David, Elijah, Gideon, Jeremiah, all 12 of Jesus's disciples and Saul of Tarsus. All were chosen before they knew it. They all were living their lives and going about their business. God decided to call them at the time He had already predestined.

Although I remember others, I only will comment on two: Samuel and Saul of Tarsus. These two Bible characters who clearly demonstrate that God chooses the person long before He calls them. My story is similar, but the Biblical narratives will validate and strengthen my story. Everyone is chosen and created for a purpose. It is such a wonderful feeling to know that you have been chosen by God. It is both beautiful and powerful to be a person with a special place in God's plan. No amount of money from an inheritance, lottery, or work, can compare to the great privilege of being chosen by God for the service of God and mankind.

The story of Samuel is found in I Samuel 3:1–18. The call from the Lord came in Chapter 3, but to appreciate Samuel's story, the chosen phenomenon, read Chapters 1 and 2.

The circumstances that led up to Samuel's conception are intriguing. First, the Lord shut up the womb of Hannah. God was up to something, and Hannah had no way of knowing this without special revelation. She simply lived her life in quiet desperation. She took it one day at a time. She looked to the Lord for the answer to her problem. Hannah used the privilege of prayer to talk, tell, reason, agonize with, propose and make a vow to the Lord. So, Hannah, the mother of Samuel, was just as much a chosen vessel as he was.

Now this story makes it abundantly clear that God has a date, time, and an hour in mind. God's blessings are not random. God is not caught by surprise. There are no emergencies or accidents that He does not see and control, allow, and limit. We see this especially in God choosing Samuel. From a young boy, Samuel grew up serving in God's temple, and because of this, he found favor with God and others.

As the omniscient Father, Creator, and Provider God made the call. He knows who, what, when, where, and why. Our Heavenly Father truly does know what is best. There is no timing better than God's timing.

So, in God's appointed time, He calls His chosen one, Samuel. He called the boy four times before he recognized it was the call of God. But God used Eli, to assist in this process. Even though we are chosen, we will need the help of others. This need for help from others has been true for my life as well.

As I was preparing for college, I, too, would be headed towards my call to ministry; I just didn't know it. I knew that going to college would help me to do and be better in life. I entered college without a clue about what I was about to encounter. I found out quickly that it was going to be nothing like I previously experienced. Although only 21 miles away, I was away from home and family for the first time in my life. I had never experienced this type of independence and freedom. No one cared or checked if I went to class or not. No one was there to tell me to get up and do my work. I was not familiar with this level of freedom. But God loved me! This is why God's love is so pivotal. It gave me the freedom to make choices and as a result, I was able to choose between the voices to follow and those I should reject. I love God for how He softly and gently guided me in choosing His way as the best way for my life.

The beginning of college life for me was as normal as it was for any other freshman. My class schedule included classes on Mondays, Wednesdays, and Fridays, for two hours each per day. Outside of my class schedule, I had free time. I stopped working temporarily. I took a leave of absence from the truck loading job. This helped me adjust to college life.

I really tuned in to the extracurricular college life well and quickly. Without delay or stumbling, I learned how to play Bid Whist. I specialized in knowing the time for meals in the cafeteria. I partied with my friends from my high school. I also studied, but only enough to pass two of three classes. I got an "I" (an "Incomplete") for the third course that I completed during the second semester. I was so thankful to God when I finished the first semester. The real miracle for me was that I finished without being thrown out.

As a result, I started praying to God to help me to be successful in college. My mother was a member of an organization named Life Study Fellowship, Inc. This organization offered special written prayers for certain situations. I requested their prayer books to help me to be successful in college. Beginning with my second semester, I remained faithful to the Life Study Fellowship prayers and continued to pray until I graduated.

The second semester I passed all my courses; however, I made a "B" in one class that was a business course. It was then that I declared business administration as a major. Yet, there were things lurking in my mind. I still wanted to be a mortician. I wanted to own my own business. I even considered going into real estate.

My second year of college was a smooth transition into more serious activities. I pledged the Alpha Phi Omega National Service Fraternity, Incorporated. I also joined the Gordon-Jenkins Pre-Theological Association and became a member of the college's newspaper staff. I had no desire to teach. At this time, I did not hear the voice of God calling me into ministry; however, 'something' was happening to me. I was becoming more disciplined. I even decided to specialize in accounting.

For the first time in my life, I started feeling that I belonged. College gave me a sense of purpose. I saw that my life was actually taking shape. I also discovered that I had a speech impediment. My pronunciations and enunciations were not up to standard. So, I got serious about practicing my speaking to improve this problem. Practicing required commitment, but it also increased my confidence and performance.

CHAPTER FOUR

CHOSEN BUT NOW CALLED

My junior year of matriculating through Benedict College was special. It was then that I heard the voice of God calling me into the ministry. This started me on a journey that I value more than life itself. I began to muse over the fact that my great uncle, Mr. Abraham "Ellis" Seawright, had made a prediction one day when I was only four years old. He said, *"Lil Boy, you gonna be a preacher one day."* Because God uses others, through the Holy Spirit, way back then my uncle knew that I was chosen.

In the Bible, the story of Saul of Tarsus will help anyone see that we are chosen before we are called or converted. There is no God like our God. He is all-wise, all-powerful, and Sovereign. He chooses us while we are yet sinners and are fighting against Him. What a mighty God we serve!

In Acts 9:1-16, we read that Saul was, *"breathing out threats against the disciples of the Lord."* He went unto the high priest and desired of him, letters to Damascus to the synagogues, that if he found any of this way, whether they were men or women, he might bring them bound unto Jerusalem. And as he journeyed, he came near to Damascus: and suddenly, there shone round about him a light from Heaven: and he fell to the earth and heard a voice saying unto him, *"'Saul, Saul, why are you persecuting Me?'"* That was the beginning of Saul's call.

Jesus commanded Saul to *"Arise and go into the city, and it shall be told you what you must do."* This same Jesus, the one who called Saul, confronted Saul's evil actions. He sent Ananias, one of His disciples, to lay hands on him, that he might receive his sight again.

Because of Saul's violent reputation that preceded him, Ananias was afraid of Saul. However, Jesus comforted him with these words in verses 15 and 16 of Acts 9:

> *"Go your way. He is a chosen vessel unto Me, to bear My name before the Gentiles, and Kings, and the children of Israel. For I will show him how great things he must suffer for My (Jesus)') name's sake. [emphasis mine]"*

Saul who eventually was renamed *Paul* by Jesus, was chosen. Paul would later speak in Galatians 1:15 about himself:

> *"But when it pleased God, who separated me (chose me) from my mother's womb, and called me by His grace, to reveal His Son in me, that I might preach Him (Jesus) among the heathen."*

I remembered by uncle's words *"Lil boy, you gonna be a preacher one day."* For me, and in the context of this chapter, the words, "one day," stand out. We see this in Acts 9. Jesus spoke this truth with clarity and authority to Saul of Tarsus on the road to Damascus. There was so much going on in Saul's life when Jesus interrupted, intervened, and imparted truth to him. Saul was lost and had become a terrorist, an enemy of Jesus the Christ and Jesus' followers.

When I was called by God, I also was active, but active in doing good things. I was trying to do my best academically. And when I wasn't in school, my plate was full performing other good works. Then, in the midst of the many things pulling on me at the time, God called me to something and someone bigger and better than anything I had ever imagined.

On the Sunday afternoon of January 23, 1977, at Prodigal AME Church in Swansea, South Carolina, before a packed congregation of family and friends, I preached my first sermon. This was an honor, a privilege, and an offering to my Savior and Lord. The joy and honor of being chosen and called by God overwhelmed my total existence. I owe it all to God and to Him, I give the glory.

When I reached my senior year at Benedict College, I was growing and going. My attitude and behavior were changing right before my eyes. I found myself developing and exercising my leadership skills. For me the highest manifestation of these significant developments was my election as president of both the Gordon-Jenkins Theological Association and the Alpha Phi Omega Fraternity, Incorporated.

Due to extenuating circumstances, to my surprise 18 months after my first sermon, I was assigned as interim pastor of St. Stephens AME Church in St. Matthews, South Carolina—the church in the same town as my former high school. During this time, I started receiving advice and encouragement from God through one of my fraternity brothers, Rev. Jerry Sanders, a minister, and Dr. Latta Thomas, a professor at Benedict College. Both Rev. Sanders and Dr. Thomas shared with me the need to consider seminary training.

As I look back, I can see the will of God being fulfilled in my life. God was most definitely in the details. The calling was great, and God was leading and guiding me. My faith in God was showing and growing. There was so much going on in my life at the age of 20, that I could hardly comprehend it all. It was also during this time that I had met Ms. Sherita Moon, who would later become my wife. The night before my initial sermon, Sherita and I went on our first date. Meeting Sherita was an answer to my prayer. I had been praying to God that He would send me a girlfriend who would become my wife. The night of our first date, when I returned to the dormitory, I told my roommate, Jerry Sanders, that I had met the *'future Mrs. Harry L. Seawright.'*

Falling in love with Sherita was ordained by God. She had such an encouraging spirit. She was a smart, straight "A" student, and disciplined. The second oldest of three siblings, (second to her brother and the oldest of her two sisters), Sherita was from a family of modest means. Her father was a preacher/pastor and her mother a schoolteacher and graduate of Benedict College. Sherita accepted me for who I was and never placed herself above me.

As I pursued the ministry and continued to fulfill the requirements for my business administration degree in accounting, I began to question whether it was a good idea to continue getting a degree in business while pursuing the ministry. My desire to operate my own business was a dream I did not want to abandon completely, but my call from God was stronger. I completed my degree in accounting and graduated from Benedict College in May 1978.

After graduation, I applied to the Interdenominational Theological Center in Atlanta, Georgia, and the Howard University School of Religion in Washington, D.C. I continued as the interim pastor at St. Stephens AME Church, St, Matthews, S.C. while waiting to hear whether I had been accepted at either school. I only applied to Howard at the urging of Dr. Thomas, my college minister. The School of Religion had gotten a new dean,

Dr. Lawrence N. Jones, and, according to Dr. Thomas, *"exciting things were happening there."*

Wherever I ended up going, it would be difficult leaving St. Stephens. I was truly enjoying being the interim pastor. I received acceptance letters and scholarships from both Howard University and the Interdenominational Theological Center. Howard University's School of Religion offered me a full scholarship, whereas the Interdenominational Theological Center only provided me with a partial scholarship. After much prayer, I informed my mother, family, my friends, Sherita, Bishop Frank M. Reid II, Rev. John L. Davis, my pastor, and the congregation of St. Stephens AME Church that I would be attending Howard.

There I was, on my way to Washington, DC, where I only knew one person, Sherita's aunt, Mrs. Josephine Oliver, whom I had only met once. My landlord at the time Mrs. Hattie Kinley asked me to look up her relatives once I arrived. What a blessing that was for me. Her relatives became good friends and pillars of support upon my arrival. In fact, until they died, we remained friends.

CHAPTER FIVE

CHOSEN, IN A MESS, but STILL BLESSED

When the time came for me to leave for Washington, DC, I found myself in a big mess. It seemed as though things began falling apart. Specifically, the funds that I needed to go to DC were not available. No one I reached out to was able to help me financially and I was ready to go! However, there was no money. But God! Yes, God was on time. God provided through my mother.

It was at this exact moment that my mother received her first disability income check with back pay from the application time. We had done our due diligence in praying. We spent time together, talking and praying. She prayed. I prayed. We reasoned with God. We questioned God! God heard our humble cry and call. When the check came, we knew it was a mighty miracle from God! God's timing is nothing short of amazing. Again, God made a way. I am still thankful and joyful for God's provisions. I am also grateful for my mother's great sacrifice.

It was because of this that I was able to leave South Carolina and start the next chapter of my life as a student in a divinity school in the nation's capital. While I knew that I was leaving a mess behind, I did not know of the trials, the tribulations, the trouble, and the tough roads ahead. However, I was chosen. I now had a college degree and that encouraged and comforted me.

I was only 22-years-old when I arrived in Washington, D.C., where I knew only one person. But I knew God! I also believed God knew me. God knew that I had limited funds. He also knew that most of the promises made by Howard University's School of Religion had not yet materialized.

I received tuition, but no room and board. This was a problem that I had to get resolved quickly. With no other options, I ended up renting a room in a boarding house that had rats the size of some of the cats I had seen living in South Carolina. I wanted to return to SC, but I had quit my job with the trucking company, and I had resigned as interim pastor of the St. Stephens AME Church. I was in a really big mess and to top it off, all of my worldly possessions could fit in one suitcase. And now I had a car note, monthly rent, and no job. I surely questioned whether I had made the right decision. But God! Yes, God waited and watched to see whether I would turn to Him for mercy.

I did turn to my precious Heavenly Father for mercy. God then started to build me a new family away from home. God's family is not limited to any little, middle, or big-sized city. His people and His servants are everywhere. His blood, fellowship, and relationship are spiritual and not limited to biological status. He sent me help from one of my divinity school classmates.

My help came from a simple invitation from Sis. Geneva Watson whose husband pastored Reid Temple AME Church that was located near the divinity school. Sometimes help often comes simply from good and timely information. Sometimes it is a hint. For the wise, a hint can be sufficient. I accepted the invitation. I immediately joined Reid Temple AME Church and met the pastor, Rev. Kearny Watson. I was then surrounded by a caring and loving congregation of people that embraced me. The pastor and his wife invited me not only to worship at church, but also to share with their family. Some of those good Reid Temple friends and relationships continue even today.

However, as wonderful as things were moving along, the big mess still existed. I am so glad that God had a plan and a process. He wanted me to be successful. He is a coach who wants what's best for every player. He wants to bring out the best in each individual. Therefore, He will not abort the process he plans. Quite often, this means the more time we spend in *the mess* when God brings us out, we appreciate the success at a greater level.

Soon after joining Reid Temple, my financial situation worsened. I was down to fifty cents per day for dinner. Thank God for McDonald's: in 1978 that fine restaurant offered fifty-cent hamburgers and a free cup of water. In addition to barely being able to feed myself, my car was about to be repossessed. But God! I needed help! But I believe God waited and watched until I *wanted* the help enough to ask for the help that was already there!

On one Sunday, I went to the altar in extreme desperation. I was so overwhelmed that I yelled out to the Lord, pleading for help. As a result of that outburst of desperation—unplanned, unrehearsed, and totally unexpected by everyone, including me—several members of Reid Temple formed a committee where each member agreed to sow into me $10 every month to help me out.

I was on my way now, growing and knowing that God's ways are not my ways. The prophet Isaiah declared, *"As high as the heavens are above the earth, so are God's thoughts above our thoughts, and His ways above our ways."* These experiences were a part of the process, but I had to press on the upward way.

I am glad to say that when I look back, I know that all things were working together for my good because I loved God and was called according to His purpose. However, it's even more wonderful and awesome when facing present-day crises, I can say, *"I know. Yes, I know that all things are working together for good for me now."* I don't have to understand. I only need to accept God's plan. I am chosen!

The kind gesture of the members of Reid Temple AME Church provided some significant financial security and enabled me to buy food, pay my car note, and provide gas money so I could look for a job. Then, fortunately, a room became available in the School of Religion's dormitory. Hallelujah! I was able to leave the rat-infested rowhouse that served me well at the start of my divinity school journey.

Because information travels fast, more improvements came. Sherita, continuing to accept me for who I was, talked to her aunt, about my situation. Her aunt followed up on our conversation talking to her friend, Mr. Carter, about my predicament. They both were graduates of Benedict College. He was a neighbor of the treasurer of the AME Church, at the time, Dr. Joseph C. McKinney and his wife Mrs. Mary Lee McKinney. Through their intervention, I met with Dr. McKinney, and he informed me that he would employ me for at least two weeks.

Dr. McKinney needed someone to work on some equipment that he had received from Kittrell College in North Carolina. Kittrell College had recently closed. After two weeks, he found more work for me to do. There were times when I emptied the trash, swept the driveway, and did other menial chores. My faith began to wane. Here I was with a college degree, and I was pushing a broom and mop to support myself. I had to keep telling myself that God was paving the way.

Several months later, he approached me and asked me to work with Allen Travel, a newly formed travel agency through the AME Church. He felt that with my business degree and accounting skills, I could do well. I started keeping the books for the travel agency, and pretty soon, I was asked to assist the bookkeeping department for the AME Church.

Remember, only a year or so earlier, I could not see the connection between a degree in business and religion. God proved to be my eyes when I could not see. Some years later, I was promoted to chief accountant and that appointment turned into 12 years of employment. By working in the finance department, I learned the inner workings of the AME Church. It was during this time that I realized that God used my most difficult moments to teach me my greatest lessons. Through divine intervention, although at a different location, the same denominational organization where I swept the floors and driveway and pulled trash is the same organization that displays my picture as the 133rd Elected and Consecrated Bishop of the African Methodist Episcopal Church.

Dr. McKinney became my mentor and a strong supporter as I worked toward a degree and my goals in ministry. As the accountant with the church's finance department, I was able to attend all the General Board meetings and General Conferences. Attending these events gave me the opportunity to meet bishops and pastors from various churches around the world, all who were affiliated with the AME Church.

I also took on the task of running errands for and transporting the bishops, their wives, the general officers, and other church officials to and from the airport, train stations, and hotels during meetings and conferences in the D.C. area. Through these encounters, I grew to have great respect and admiration for the bishops, general officers, and other dignitaries, especially the ones I had an opportunity to work alongside.

During these years, I could not initially see that God was ordering my every step. But God did for me exactly what He did for Abraham: He allowed me and my faith to grow. And then one day, through my own personal *messy* experiences, I came to know God's presence and power in the time of the storm. God made a way out of no way for me, and I came to learn and appreciate the fact that all we must do is get out of the way and obey.

"Nothing beats a failure, but a try." I often heard these words spoken by my mother during my childhood and upbringing. In my frequent phone calls to my mother, she constantly reminded me of how much she was praying for me. I was strengthened and encouraged by her faith. I soon realized that many, many people were praying for me.

Reid Temple AME continued to be a springboard for my life. I was surrounded by strong, faith-filled people whom I honor today for their love and support. Because of the prayers and outpouring of support from people I did not know and my mother's words ringing in my ears, I could not give up. I had to keep trying! I soon came to love the scripture found in Galatians 6:9:

"And let us not become weary in well doing: for in due season, we shall reap, if we faint not."

You know God is truly, truly awesome. One year later, after living in a rat-infested boarding house, with only fifty cents for dinner, I was offered an assistant pastor's position at Pilgrim

AME Church in Washington, DC. I was welcomed with open arms by the pastor, The Reverend James Robinson, and his wonderful wife, Mrs. Linda Robinson.

The Pilgrim AME Church family was supportive, encouraging, and nurturing. As an assistant pastor, I worked along with the church administrator, overseeing the financial operations of the church. I also accompanied the pastor to visit the sick and shut-in and performed other duties as assigned. When Reverend Robinson was transferred to Ward Memorial AME—the home church of my mentor, Dr. McKinney—I continued to serve as the assistant pastor to the newly assigned Pastor at Pilgrim, The Reverend Gregory Edmond.

Rev. Edmond immediately became my family away from home. He and his wife, Mrs. Mary Edmond were extremely kind to me, and their sons, Andre and Patrick became my little brothers. When my funds ran out and I could not pay tuition, room, and board for my last semester at Howard, they opened up their home to me. I joyfully and gratefully moved in with them, until I finished my degree. Additionally, during these lean financial times, Dr. McKinney gave me the hope and assistance I needed to complete my last semester of seminary training. My faith was further strengthened in the fact that *"If God be for us, who can be against us?" (Romans 8:31b)*

Today, I praise God for the people who saw something in me when I could not see anything in myself. I am indeed grateful for the friends I met in seminary and the different churches I was fortunate enough to be a member. In many instances, pastors invited me to preach at the churches where they served. Several of them provided love offerings that were of great assistance in providing needed funds for survival.

Two pastors in particular invited me often, the late Reverend William R. Porter of Hemingway Memorial AME Church, then in Chapel Oaks, Maryland, and the Reverend Dessie Carter of Embry AME Church, College Park, Maryland. Even today, some of these churches and parishioners still contact me to preach at their churches. I have been blessed. God knows I have been.

I say to any person who is wondering about the possibilities of life, please remember that God has a purpose and plan. God's purpose and plan are expanded by the number of steps we are willing to take. I echo the words of Iyanla Vanzant in her book, *Value in the Valley*: *"When we step out, the universe will start to participate on our behalf."*

Difficulties and circumstances will arise; that's life, but keep remembering this fact: *"You, dear children, are from God and have overcome them because the one who is in you is greater than the one in the world" (1 John 4:4).* You will never even know what you can accomplish until you try. The late retired Colonel, Reverend Lee Cousin, who served on the ministerial staff at one of the churches I pastored, would often say, *"Go ahead and jump off the cliff. You just might fly."* I add that if God is telling you to do so, "jump." He will give you wings. In the words of Mama, *"Nothing beats a failure, but a try."*

CHAPTER SIX

CHOSEN Path, Place, and Position

Faith to believe in God and all His possibilities, the faith of a praying mother, and faith from within, are all powerful tools. The unshakable love of family, friends, a devoted wife, children, and a grandchild keeps me going. Having unshakable faith is a survival skill, especially for those of us who are Black.

In the small rural town in South Carolina where I grew up, racism was real. I encountered it on a daily basis. Blacks were able to survive as long as we stayed *in our place*. Those who decided to test their fate were dealt with accordingly. As a young man, I heard the horror stories about Blacks who didn't know their (immorally ascribed) place. There were stories of Blacks being lynched, the homes of Blacks being burned to the ground, and Blacks fleeing to the North to keep from being killed by racist Whites.

I believe my Heavenly Father made many choices for me and at the same time, He allowed me the opportunity to make many choices for myself. He did choose my parents. He chose the continent, the state, the county, and the city in which I was born and reared. However, I had to choose to grow, to be developed, trained, and prepared to become a greater servant of the Most High God from this lowly and obscure place, Swansea, S.C., as the son of sharecroppers to being a Son of God!

For me, Swansea was a place of humble beginnings, and it reminds me of another place of humble beginnings, Bethlehem Ephrathah. Jesus, Emmanuel, the Christ from the tribe of Judah, was born there. When looking at Jesus's journey, it seems the smaller, the better for the Almighty God I serve. God would take me as I was and grow me into a believer, a person of faith—from small faith to great faith over time. My life would become an awesome adventure in trusting Him. (That's faith).

My personal faith walk started in my immediate family. My father and mother were people of faith. While I only knew my father for the first five years of my life, the seed of faith was already planted to include his influence. It simply needed to be watered and nurtured. My mother demonstrated her faith by precept and example. She had a good word, a right word, and corresponding action as a clincher.

Because of the prevalence of racism, the Black church became a focal point in the Black community to combat this plague in society. The church was not only the place where we went to worship on Sundays and attend Wednesday night Bible study and prayer meetings, it was a place where the Civil Rights Movement flourished. It became the gathering place when Blacks needed to organize.

My hometown church, Prodigal AME, was a pivotal force in my life. It was worshiping and fellowshipping at Prodigal that laid the foundation of Christian doctrines upon which I continue to espouse today. It was and still is today a family church. Prodigal's membership is made of families from the surrounding communities. At this place everyone was caring, and, at times, some members were overly aggressive and competitive, especially when it came to choosing leaders in the church. These types of "church fights" were not often, but they did annoy my spirit.

Nevertheless, Prodigal Church helped mold and shape me into the person I am today. Young people always had a role in the church. We were encouraged to participate in the choir and Sunday school. For every religious holiday, we had to learn and say a speech or participate in the church play. I was the first person in over two decades to enter the ministry from my church. As I left for college, the church family showed how proud they were of me by giving me money to purchase my books.

On the second Wednesday in August of 1969 at the age of 13, I was saved at the *mourner's bench.* For those who might not know, the mourner's bench was a pew, an altar or chair in the front of the church. After a sermon, especially during revivals, people who wanted to repent of their sins and ask Jesus to save them would occupy the mourner's bench. Encouraged and supported by an older adult or preacher, the seeker prayed until they felt Jesus's presence in their spirit. On the night I was saved the preacher was Bishop Nehemiah Rhinehart. He and his wife, Mother Wilhelmina Rhinehart of the Solid Rock Full Gospel Ministries of Washington, D.C., returned to their native hometown of Swansea for our annual revival. On that hot summer night, I made a commitment to follow Jesus. Since that time I have been on the battlefield fighting for the cause of Christ.

My love for the God's church kept me in the church. I was greatly encouraged to participate in church activities by the Sunday School Superintendent who also was one of my first Sunday school teachers, the late Julia B. Geiger. This strong woman of faith taught others and me the value of serving and doing God's work. By example, she urged us to place our lives in God's hands. My cousin Marguerite Seawright, who was also a Sunday school teacher, always took me and other young people of the church to Sunday School Conventions, exposing us to other churches and opening doors for other possibilities.

My love for the church was matched by my love of gospel music. As a young man, when I had money, I would order gospel records through the mail. I grew up listening to gospel quartets: the spirit-filled voices of Edna Gallmon Cooke, Mahalia Jackson, Rev. James Cleveland, and one of my all-time favorite songbirds, Pastor Shirley Caesar. Gospel music spoke to my spirit and gave me the extra boost I needed to keep pressing forward. To me, the music spoke to my pain and disappointment, helped me cope with the things I could not change, and gave me the strength to believe in the possibilities of God. It was my soul's food and the fuel I needed to get to the next level of godliness.

Growing up fatherless and poor, I tried to live a saved life. That proved to be a major struggle for me. At the age of 18, I became a trustee at my church and president of the Lay Organization at the same time. I remember older members of the congregation telling me that I could do it. Even back then, in the back of my mind, I believed that God was preparing me for the ministry. At that time, I never had the courage or the encouragement to honestly think about it. Prior to getting accepted to college, I had resigned myself to being a good church member and working as a plumber.

In growing up and going through puberty, dating, trying to understand the importance of life, overcoming fears faced during adolescence, fighting with my brothers and peers, and maintaining my sanity, I owe my survival to a wonderful God. I remember praying that God would bring me through these years mired in confusion. During these, "wonder years," I developed a thirst to learn more about my race.

I started going to my high school library and checking out books on great Black leaders and writers covering the

Black experience. I read about Booker T. Washington, George Washington Carver, Thurgood Marshall, and Mary McLeod Bethune. I soon began to learn about Historically Black Colleges and Universities (HBCUs); during that time, they were labeled UNCF (United Negro College Fund) schools.

I never will forget the day I picked up a college manual and became fascinated by the history of Howard University. I could hardly believe there was a Black university in the United States with a Law School, a School of Religion, and a Medical School offering opportunities for Black students. I believe a seed was sown that day. I am forever grateful that an internal flame was ignited. As I read about Howard University, I had no idea that one day I would earn two degrees from that wonderful institution.

When God's hands are on your life, there is no secret to what He can and will do. My love for books took me to unknown worlds, but at the same time, caused me to become withdrawn from family and friends. I found myself marching to a different drumbeat. I would rather stay home and read a book than go to a party, a movie with friends, or a family outing. It was also during my adolescent years that I read the entire New Testament of *The Holy Bible*.

I slept with a map of the world on the wall next to my bunk bed. Between the ages of 16 and 18, I would look at that map and dream of places I wanted to go. As of this writing, on six different occasions, I have been to the "Motherland" in South Africa, West Africa, and East Africa. I have traveled to Europe, Canada, Mexico, South America, the Caribbean Islands, and almost all states in the United States. What a mighty God we serve!

I was considered by many to be a model student during high school and received the *Student Citizenship Award* at my high school graduation in 1974. I was told it was the highest nonacademic award that a student could receive. I felt honored then, and I continue to cherish that recognition today.

CHAPTER SEVEN

CHOSEN to Suffer and to Soar

(Part I)

It is both necessary and essential to know certain things in life in order to be equipped to handle bigger, better, harder, more complex, and more rewarding things. Yes, I know it, even when at certain times and circumstances, I don't show it. In those same circumstances, God gets the glory. God is faithful despite our sins of commission or omission. Jesus showed us this when He faithfully, graciously, and lovingly restored Peter despite his awful denial of Jesus.

I love the hymn, *Great Is Thy Faithfulness* because it reinforces the concept of God's faithfulness as only great lyrics and music can do for the human soul. Singing great songs and reading great lyrics, poems, and books are essential for spiritual growth. Reading the biographies of great men and women who overcame unimaginable odds to reach greater success also demonstrates the faithfulness of God. Whether in sickness and health, sorrow and gladness, pain, and joy, as well as through sufferings and victories, we can trust God. God is faithful in good times, as He is faithful when times are difficult. We must not allow the troubles of this life to cause us to forget that God is faithful. And God is faithful, all the time!

This chapter is filled with issues - my physical health issues. I have dealt with heart attacks, chest pain, blocked arteries, gallbladder removal, and the real pressures of being a real dad to two small children while my wife was away dealing with her mom's death.

All at the same time leading a congregation through a church construction program. Yet, in the midst of all of this, God was faithful. He is faithful, and He will always be faithful regardless of the circumstance.

In May 1981 when I graduated from Howard School of Religion, I received a Distinguished Student Award, Titled, "The Student most likely to excel in the Pastoral Ministry". In the same month I received my first pastoral appointment by Bishop John Hurst Adams. My first church was Payne Memorial AME in Jessup, Maryland. I was filled with irrepressible joy. I was wholly and fully committed to giving God my best! Determination and zeal defined me. I married my college sweetheart within nine months of my appointment. We had challenges, but we also had no fear. Perfect love casts out all fear!

Throughout its 87-year-old history, Payne Memorial had been without indoor plumbing but in 18 months, God demonstrated His faithfulness. The members had a mind to work. They were beautiful, cooperative, and caring.

God's faithfulness shone through brightly in the earnestness of the members in a dark hour when we suffered the miscarriage of our first child. As traumatic as the loss of our child was, we were not defeated. A few months later, Sherita was pregnant again. This was a practical way of God laying a rock-solid foundation for years to come. I am convinced that God allows the setbacks, to arrange the set up for a strong, God-orchestrated comeback.

After two years at Payne Memorial, Bishop Adams appointed me to my second pastoral appointment at Hemingway Temple AME Church. An inner-city church located in the heart of Washington, DC, the nation's capital, which offered many opportunities for ministry. Although the congregation was made of many people in their retirement years, those people were excited about serving and wanted the best for their church. Their children, grandchildren, and other family members joined them and made the experience well worth the effort.

At this point in my life and career, the farthest thing from my mind was becoming a Bishop in the African Methodist Episcopal Church. I was satisfied being the best husband, father, and pastor that I could be in whatever field I labored. Unlike Ruth who *happed*, (Bible language for happened), upon the field of Boaz, I wasn't searching for a new field—overtly or covertly. I was taking one day at a time. My life still had ups and then downs. I ascribe it to the sine curve on the medical monitor indicating life or death. But God was at work, preparing me for the day when He would call me to pursue the office and service of a bishop.

At my second appointment I went from seeing a small success to experiencing major progress. When I arrived, the church already had a thriving ministry of feeding the homeless every Wednesday. We strengthened that ministry by providing personal hygiene bags to the homeless and offering free income tax preparations during tax season. We paid down the debt of the church. We also worked relentlessly to increase membership through door-to- door evangelism.

As a church, and through teamwork, we installed air conditioning and new carpet. I was determined to give God my best. However, to my disappointment, the membership did not grow as anticipated. We even tried to relocate the church to a Maryland suburb in hopes of expansion, but that failed. Ultimately, lack of support and lack of funds brought unfortunate failure. I was disappointed!

Not relocating the church presented me with my first major setback in pastoral ministry. I wondered where was God? God was there. He was still Jehovah Shammah, the one who saw the beginning and the end. He superintends. And I believe that way back then, God knew how, where, and when this lowly experience would transcend.

I felt defeated! My faith began to diminish, and self-doubt set in and overwhelmed me. I seriously contemplated walking away from the ministry. I enrolled at the University of the District of Columbia (UDC) to pursue a degree in mortuary service. My troubles temporarily triumphed over me. Yet, God allowed it to build spiritual muscle for me to soar. As I heard it from another believer, *"The heavier the load, the stronger the faith."* The Lord knew what He had in mind in due time; I did not. So, I could only take one day at a time.

I still testify that God was truly faithful to me at one of my lowest points. I was living out a verse in Proverbs 14:12: *"There is a way that seems right unto a man, but the end of that way is death."* As I look back, I can only imagine The Spirit of God saying,

"Seek ye the Lord while He may be found, call you upon Him while He is near: Let the wicked forsake his way and the unrighteous man his thoughts, and let him return unto the Lord, and He, (God), will have mercy on him, for He will abundantly pardon him. For my thoughts are not your thoughts, neither are your ways my ways, saith the Lord. For as high as the heavens are above the earth, so are my ways higher than your ways and my thoughts than your thoughts." (Isaiah 55:6-7)

So, my God shook me out of my temporary contentment. I was not expecting this because my wife had a great government job and income. We were expecting our second child, a boy. And I was almost finished with mortuary school. But God! My ever-loving, ever-faithful God saw me drifting in the wrong direction. Instead of rejection, which I deserved, I was elevated to an unexpected new pastoral assignment again by Bishop Adams, that would last for the next 30 years and provide the platform and springboard for me, at the 2016 General Conference, to become the 133rd bishop elected and consecrated in the African Methodist Episcopal Church.

God moved again. Union Bethel AME Church in Brandywine, Maryland was the site of my third pastoral assignment. I only knew a little about the church, mostly that it was a family church. However, God was moving. He was sending me to a church that would reignite my enthusiasm and my passion for ministry. This church was ripe and ready for growth. It was God's plan. However, I did not have a clue about all God was up to...but I was excited again!

CHAPTER EIGHT

CHOSEN to Suffer and to Soar

(Part II)

We got off to a great start at Union Bethel AME Church. Dr. Walter L. Hildebrand, the presiding elder, and the members immediately informed me of their desire to build a new church. We all understood what a mighty task this would be, but by trusting God we went full steam ahead. I had no idea it would take us approximately five years to complete this project and to see this God-size dream fulfilled.

The building kick-off was great! Excitement was in the air. We established planning committees, building committees, and fundraising. We hired an architect, engineers, contractors, consultants, and engaged volunteers. God's grace towards us was amazing. The church membership started expanding. We now had a significant number of new members that embraced the vision: *A NEW CHURCH!*

Erecting a new building does not eliminate the pastor's role to minister to the sheep in the fold. So, I continued to visit the sick and perform all the pastoral responsibilities, as needed. Until one day, I needed medical attention.

Two months before the construction commenced on the edifice, I was hospitalized. I underwent surgery to have my gallbladder removed. Life was reminding me that there was no gain without some corresponding pain. This was a painful lesson on practicing what you preach. I was overloaded and in the habit of over-extending. After I recovered, I resigned from my accounting position at the AME Church's Financial Department.

Sherita's mother passed away after several months of being ill. While her travels and absences multiplied the load on our young family, the church construction project brought a new obstacle: the construction had stopped on the church. The church had no more money and the contractor walked off the work site after we failed to meet those financial demands. Then the straw that broke the camel's back was my own insufficiency to care for my children while my wife was gone to be with her mother. I cried! I was ready to throw in the towel. But God!

God provided me with a human confidante, the Rev. Dr. C. Anthony Muse. He listened! He responded. He told me to get in his car. He drove me to the church's construction site. He stood in the middle of the site in mud and water. He then prayed with me. I will never forget one line from that prayer. He said, "God is able to complete that which He has started." God was faithful! Within one week, God touched the hearts of the church members, and we raised the $12,000 needed to resume construction.

If it was not one thing, it was another, before we reached our milestone. The contractors were now functioning but in unbelief. They said, *"There is no way that the dedication [would] occur on July 14, 1991."* Working, walking, and watching by sight made them sound right. But "without faith, it is impossible to please God." I remained steadfast, unshakable, and unmovable that the dedication date would take place on the day that God had given me.

I am convinced that, "No good thing will God withhold from those who walk uprightly." When I went to the Southern

Maryland Electric Company to share our dilemma with them, I had no idea what God would do. Our dilemma was that the church had no doors, no carpet, no electricity, and, again, no money. With the scheduled dedication set for less than one week away, God used Ms. Mary Adams, an employee of the electric company, to rescue us. She became God's instrument to expedite the process of the church getting electricity. She later became a member of Union Bethel AME Church.

We worked! We worked together. We all saw God stand with us, His provisions for us as He demonstrated that He would always be faithful to us.

The dedication ceremonies of the new Union Bethel AME Church were held at 10:00 am and 3:30 pm on July 14, 1991, the date that God placed on my heart. Little did I know about another date in the distant future. God already had bigger and better plans for an elaborate, illustrious ceremony for a lowly servant from a lowly state, to be elected a bishop and receive, *"THE PURPLE ROBE" on July 11th and consecrated on July 13, 2016.*

In the meantime, there were more hills and valleys, trials, tribulations, and temptations. Sanctification is a process of a lifetime. There was a process in place. God was leading me, surely and safely. I had to walk by faith, not by sight. I had to wait on God. But the enemy called fatigue showed up and showed out. I was burned out. I started feeling a sense of uselessness. Things seemed to start going haywire for me. I felt a gigantic sense of emptiness. Thank God for loving and caring ministers whom God used to help me through with intercessory prayer when I needed it most.

In spite of everything I was going through, I actually believed my purpose was fulfilled. I thought there was nothing left for me to do. But God had more in store. He had another chore for me. I was only 38. And like Moses, only God knew about all the tests, sufferings, and life-threatening challenges I would face.

I decided to enroll in the doctoral program at Howard University Divinity School. Studying was good for me. But the life of pastoring, supporting a family and a growing suburban church on the outskirts of the nation's capital had its own unique and inherent demands. There were bittersweet moments and so many struggles that made me wonder about my purpose. I even questioned God about why I was given so many tests of my faith.

In conjunction with my doctoral studies, I also began working as a fellow with the Congress of National Black Churches Fellowship Program for Pastors at Partners for Sacred Places, Incorporated in Philadelphia, Pennsylvania. I was completing my final semester of coursework towards my Doctor of Ministry Degree and was ready to celebrate when I faced another major hurdle.

In December 1994, while walking the streets of Philadelphia, I began having severe chest pains. I was rushed to a local hospital. They discovered one of my main arteries had a 90% blockage. Amazingly though, I was informed that x-rays revealed that I was born with three main arteries; normally people have only two. Only one in a million are born with three main arteries, they told me. The pressure of the blocked arteries should have caused a massive heart attack, but God was faithful. The heart attack was prevented because my body was fearfully and wonderfully made with an extra artery! I had all the symptoms of a massive heart attack, but there was no damage to my heart. Praise the Lord!

This was a serious and exciting time in my life. I chose to "Trust in the Lord with all my heart and lean not to my own understanding," *(Proverbs 3:5-7).* In all my ways I acknowledged Him, and the Lord directed my path. I chose to not be wise in my own eyes, but to fear God and depart from evil.

A month later, in January 1995, I underwent an angioplasty procedure and had a stent implanted in the blocked artery. The night before the surgery, I found solace in Psalm 30:1 – 6*:*

I will exalt You, LORD, for You lifted me out of the depths and did not let my enemies gloat over me. LORD my God, I called to You for help, and You healed me. You, LORD, brought me up from the realm of the dead; You spared me from going down to the pit. Sing the praises of the LORD, you his faithful people; praise HIS holy name. For HIS anger lasts only a moment, but HIS favor lasts a lifetime; weeping may stay for the night, but rejoicing comes in the morning. When I felt secure, I said, "I will never be shaken."

During the surgical procedure, the angioplasty balloon pierced the artery and caused uncontrollable bleeding. After six hours, the surgeons finally stopped the bleeding. I was placed in intensive care for several days. According to experts most people would not have survived the uncontrollable bleeding during heart surgery. I knew then that God was with me. EMMANUEL! The Lord is my Shepherd. Even though I walked through the valley of the shadow of death, I feared no evil. God had a plan for me. I believed it! I knew it! God was miraculously showing it!

All of this happened for a purpose and yet there was more to come. I believed that God wanted me to know for sure that His Word, His promises are sure, strong, and true. Writing my doctoral project under these special circumstances was stressful, tedious, and challenging. Yet, God's grace was sufficient. I developed a daily routine of writing, working out on the treadmill, and taking short walks outside. This was both a humbling and demanding time of my life. As I increased my daily Bible reading, my faith increased while my physical strength and health gradually improved. I was back on track and ready to finish the doctoral journey. I had no idea what else would go wrong.

The Thursday before graduation, I was out taking a walk. About three blocks from my house, a severe pain ripped through my chest. I started having shortness of breath. I was sweating and feeling tired. I stopped walking, regained my composure, and proceeded to walk a little farther. I made it home and drove myself to the doctor. God was truly my refuge, a present help in another time of trouble. God was up to something bigger. God wanted absolute, unwavering faith and dependence on Him and His word.

I was diagnosed with having another heart attack because the stent that was implanted earlier in January blocked off. I was transferred to Georgetown University Hospital where I underwent a second procedure to unblock the stent. This caused me to spend the day in intensive care. The bleeding had not stopped.

I declare that my God's strength is made perfect in weakness. He wanted to show this to the world. But He needed a weak and humble vessel through whom He would operate, if only they would cooperate.

I had a major dilemma! But did I? God's Word said, *"The things which are impossible to man are possible with God."* My graduation was scheduled for Saturday and here I was, on

Thursday night, lying in a hospital bed in the ICU. I told the doctors, nurses, and everyone else who would listen, about my dilemma. However, the bleeding continued. My hope of getting to my graduation was bleak. The praying continued with my wife, family, friends, and church members staying the course of intercessory prayer.

Finally, on Friday, the doctor said to me, "If your bleeding stops in one hour, I will release you to attend your graduation." This was around 4:00 pm. By 5:00 pm, the doctor said to me, "If you continue not bleeding, you can go home by 6:00 pm." At 6:00 pm, I was released directly from the ICU to go home. I was weak but excited.

I watched the on-campus Howard University graduation on television from home. Sherita hooded me with the other students as family members watched, including my mother, my children, my sister, her husband, and other family members from New York.

Sherita had borrowed a wheelchair from the church, and she helped me to the car and drove me to Washington, DC so that I could participate in the Divinity School's graduation ceremony. There at the graduation, several things happened. I was awarded the 1995 Doctor of Ministry (D. Min.) degree and the Student of the Year award for outstanding doctoral project. Evangelist Shirley Caesar's husband, the late Bishop Harold Williams, was a part of my graduating class. While laying hands on me she prayed. Not only was I at my graduation, my favorite gospel singer ministered to me! I was on cloud nine.

During the awarding of degrees, a member of Union Bethel Bro. French Thompson pushed me to the stage in my wheelchair.

I walked across the stage and receives my D. Min. degree. The audience erupted in applause. I shall never forget that day of triumph and victory. I know the power of prayer is real, and I know God answers prayer. I hung on to the prayers of people like Pastor Grainger Browning, who preached at my 39th birthday celebration. He said, "You will march in May." I felt the prayers of people around the country, if not the world.

I had to recuperate for another six months. During that time, I stayed in the God's word daily. Bro. Kevin Carter, a good friend who is like a brother, was unemployed at the time. To help my mental state, Kevin would pick me up in the mornings and drive me all over Maryland, discovering new places, riding boats, and even fishing. The time passed quickly. Sherita remained steadfast and committed. I had to change my diet, continuously exercise, and relax.

The glorious part about my medical dilemma is that I never experienced heart damage. This is how I know that even when we go through different seasons in life, some good and some bad, God is faithful. Through it all, I am a witness that whatever God takes us to, He is more than able to bring us through.

CHAPTER NINE

CHOSEN but JUST DO IT AGAIN

At the time, this book is being written, there are now between 7.5 to 8.0 billion people alive on the face of the earth. However, it all started with one man and one woman. But most importantly, this enormous population started with one God, the Creator Almighty, who is all-seeing and knowing, everywhere present and eternal: past, present, and future, the One True God. What a mighty God we serve!

After continuous prayer in June 2006, I kept hearing God say, *"More."* I asked Him repeatedly, *"God what do You want me to do?"*

On Pentecost Sunday in June 2006, I woke up as usual at 5:45 a.m., prayed, read my devotional materials and the daily scriptures from the *The One Year Bible*. I read 1 Timothy 3:1: *"And this is a true saying. He who desires the office of a bishop desires a good work."* That scripture resonated with me.

People had predicted that I would preach one day. Others were more specific. At seminary my colleagues called me "Bishop". They prophesied that I would be a bishop also, one day. I vividly remember six months after preaching my initial sermon, being the guest pastor for a youth day service at an AME Church in Orangeburg, South Carolina. An older gentleman suddenly jumped from his seat. He ran across the church shouting and pointed at me. "You are going to be a bishop!" He repeated this several times. I heard him, but being a bishop was not on my mind.

The journey from pastor to bishop happened between 2006 and 2016. It culminated as I was elected the 133rd Bishop in the African Methodist Episcopal Church. If I knew then, what I know now, I would have repeated the words of Jesus in the Garden of Gethsemane in Matthew 26:39:

"Oh, my Father, if it be possible, let this cup pass from me: nevertheless, not as I will, but as You will."

This journey is written so that God's name may be magnified, His will identified, and His awesome power be glorified.

God had prepared me for this day. He said, *"I led you this way. I will be with you all the way. Let's go! You must remember the truth. I am the potter; you are the clay. I will mold you and make you after My will, while you are waiting, working, watching, hoping, and trusting, yielded and still."*

I love it when God gives me confirmation—quickly. On that same pivotal Pentecost Sunday 2006, the Holy Spirit kept urging me to seek the office of the Bishop in the AME Church. I had not shared this with anyone, not even my wife. After church, my wife and two of my sons in the ministry Reverends Reginald Crump and Derrick Brown stated that they needed to talk with me. Because I just knew something bad was happening at Union Bethel, I asked them what was wrong. They agreed to tell me at dinner.

As we ate, my curiosity got the best of me. So I asked why they needed to talk with me. To my surprise, they said. *"We feel in our spirit that you need to consider running to become a bishop."* My mouth flew open, and I began to laugh. "My God, how did they know?" I thought. Then I told them that I had been asking God to show me a sign and direct my path as to what He wanted me to do next. That moment sealed my candidacy to become a bishop at the 2008 General Conference. I must be honest and admit the truth. I had a whole lot more to learn about God's ways and my heart.

From the onset, I ran a well-organized, impressive, and successful campaign with great volunteers helping and finances. We gave it our best. Yet, this was a test, the initial stress and success test. At the time, it appeared as if the odds were heavily against me to be elected during this General Conference Session. I was disappointed that I was not elected in 2008, but not disappointed in God. This was clearly a prime-time set-up for making the most of a solid setback.

I learned on the big stage and in the big performance an extremely important lesson: God's delay is not God's denial. This was a crucial lesson that God allowed me to experience in the big game of life, not on the practice field. He may not come when we want Him, but He is always right on time. There is great opportunity, however, for learning during a losing season. The loss was not to be despised. It was to make me wiser.

I am eternally grateful that I followed God's plan for me. I had a new appreciation for God's Word and this scripture (I Thessalonians 5:18) became more alive *"In everything give thanks, for this is the will of God in Christ Jesus concerning you,"*.

I simply had to practice what I preached. I accepted God's challenge for me, and in accepting that challenge, I was able to meet so many wonderful, kind, and supportive people from around the world. I had the opportunity to chair a mission trip to South Africa with a group of 33 participants. Seeking the position of a bishop helped me to know and grow exponentially, including spiritually, personally, professionally, and in my marriage and family.

God, in the midst of my pursuit of being elected as an AME bishop, had more work for me to do at Union Bethel AME Church. That work started with me, the pastor, and my immediate family. A few months after the election, Sherita experienced an illness that required my undivided attention. There were other family issues that rose to the surface that had to be dealt with. Then the church family began facing some unique challenges that God's wisdom chose to have me, rather than a new pastor, deal with. So, not being elected in 2008 was not a bad idea after all. God knew what He was doing.

Four years later in 2012, I became a candidate for bishop the second time. The 49th Session of the General Conference of the AME Church was held in Nashville, Tennessee. I put my trust in God again. I rested in the blessed assurance that God knew what was best for me. I campaigned faithfully and prepared wonderfully for the General Conference.

I trusted God to order my steps. I stood on the promises and power of God. I prayed without ceasing that God would raise up God-fearing people to pray for me and support my campaign with funding and volunteerism. Nevertheless, in 2012 I was not elected again. For the second time, I suffered defeat, but not destruction. The scripture that came to mind was, *"God is able to do exceeding abundantly above all that we can ask or think according to the power that works within us." (Ephesians 3:20).*

So, I dug deeper into the Word of God and was able to encourage myself in the Lord. I refused to become weary in well doing. I resisted the devil's attacks and lies. I resolved to wait on the Lord. Psalms 27 became precious to me and powerful for me, starting at verse 7 and through verse 14. I earnestly believed I would see the salvation and the goodness of the Lord in my lifetime:

> "*Hear, O LORD, when I cry with my voice: have mercy also upon me, and answer me. When thou saidst, Seek ye MY face; my heart said unto thee, THY face, LORD, will I seek. Hide not thy face far from me; put not THY servant away in anger: THOU hast been my help; leave me not, neither forsake me, O God of my salvation. When my father and my mother forsake me, then the LORD will take me up. Teach me thy way, O LORD, and lead me in a plain path, because of mine enemies. Deliver me not over unto the will of mine enemies: for false witnesses are risen up against me, and such as breathe out cruelty. I had fainted, unless I had believed to see the goodness of the LORD in the land of the living. Wait on the LORD: be of good courage, and HE shall strengthen thine heart: wait, I say, on the LORD.*"

In May 2013 I restarted the campaign engine and got the campaign wheels turning again. When I met with two presiding elders about my candidacy, they reported that, *"No one is really calling your name."* I told them thank you and responded in prayer. *"Lord, please help me do the right thing."* And before the month ended, I had an encouraging and uplifting meeting with the presiding prelate of my Episcopal District, Bishop William P. DeVeaux, Sr., the 113th elected Bishop of the AME Church.

Bishop DeVeaux made no verbal commitment at this time to me, but he expressed gladness for my desire to become a bishop. He even made a significant financial contribution to Seawright for Bishop (SFB). I continued to meet with key people throughout the church. The sentiment was clear. Although I had considered becoming a presiding elder, it would be counterproductive. It would shift my base support and confuse the emotions of the people. I remember having another conversation with someone who declared to me, *"You have put too much into SFB to change to Presiding Elder." "Lord, let your will be done,"* was my prayer.

This was still early in the campaign process that would run to July 2016. However, getting the sparks that would eventually start fires burning was important. I was also told by one of my sons in ministry that according to his presiding elder, my name was not being called as one of those to be elected. I responded quickly that people not calling my name (as a serious candidate for bishop) did not matter as long as God was calling my name. I prayed that God will hear my prayer.

By October 2013, I was feeling challenged in my passion and desire to be a bishop. I was involved in a conference call with fellow candidates. And while it went ok, it was definitely a time of trouble for me. I attended the Deliverance Conference in the Second Episcopal District. I felt bad that I was not on the program and as a result, I started feeling tired and unappreciated. I was also feeling inadequate, frustrated, and fearful. Things were challenging, and I was a little discouraged with myself and ministry. My earnest cry became, "Help me, Dear Lord."

God intervened October 23, 2013. A bishop gave me a large check for SFB for a reception I hosted at our Episcopal District's Mid-Year Conference. I praised God for this bishop's support. Then things took a decisive, pivotal change for the better. We had an SFB planning meeting at the Hilton Baltimore Washington International (BWI). This meeting was for district leadership. At this point, we raised a total of $6,000. I was declared the only candidate from my Episcopal District. I became rejuvenated! "God is awesome," is all I could say.

In November 2013, I attended a fall Convocation that went well. I remember riding along with some of the other pastors and elders. It was brought up in conversation that the AME Church was now talking about lowering the number of bishops to be elected. The information caught my attention and strengthened my faith. I prayed, "Lord no matter how many will be elected, let me be one of them".

The calendar year was moving toward an end, and I wanted to have a good end to the kick-off phase of my campaign for 2016. But faith comes by hearing and not only faith, but so does fear. Fear set in because somebody informed me that another pastor from our Episcopal District was planning to run for bishop. Because of my own innate fears and insecurities, my immediate appeal was to Almighty God. *"Lord, please help me, and show me the way."*

The next morning, I woke up feeling a little apprehensive about my chances of being elected. But God! The Spirit of God led me to Romans 4:17 – 25:

"As it is written: "I have made you a father of many nations." He is our father in the sight of God, in whom he believed-the God who gives life to the dead and calls into being things that were not. Against all hope, Abraham in hope believed and so became the father of many nations, just as it had been said to him, "So shall your offspring be." Without weakening in his faith, he faced the fact that his body was as good as dead-since he was about a hundred years old-and that Sarah's womb was also dead. Yet he did not waver through unbelief regarding the

promise of God, but was strengthened in his faith and gave glory to God, being fully persuaded that God had power to do what he had promised. This is why "it was credited to him as righteousness." The words "it was credited to him" were written not for him alone, but also for us, to whom God will credit righteousness for us who believe in HIM who raised Jesus our LORD from the dead. He was delivered over to death for our sins and was raised to life for our justification."

Now I was trusting in the promises of God and that I would believe and be elected bishop in 2016. His promise to me gave me assurance. I was believing in the hope of God.

As December arrived, I was still looking, hoping, and believing God for a strong finish of the 2013 calendar year. I could only take one day at a time. I knew that I could not hurry God. I really wanted Him to speed up. But God always knows what's best.

On December 29, 2013, my home church Prodigal AME lifted a love offering of $2,500.00 for me. That was followed by another offering by a couple I knew and loved, which was $2,000. This was real and serious encouragement. I prayed. *"Thank you, Father. You are my provider. Please continue to give me favor in Jesus's name."*

In February of 2014, Seawright for Bishop held a Founder's Day Dinner at Reid Temple AME Church in Glenn Dale, Maryland. I received a wonderful turnout of supporters. We served over 300 people and raised $5,000. This was encouraging! I praised the Lord! Then I got the word, the sobering word. It was confirmed that another pastor was in fact launching his campaign for bishop. He said to me, *"I am planning to announce my candidacy in April at my Annual Conference."* My response was simple. *"Lord help me to stay focused on my calling. I felt encouraged and even more determined to go forward, in Jesus's name."*

On April 24, 2014, the other pastor kept his word and announced his candidacy to become a bishop at the 2016 General Conference of the AME Church. The next day a bishop comforted me by referring me to Romans 4:17-25. He said, *"God's promises are strong in the area of impossibilities. Be strong in faith."* This was more than comforting. It was also confirming. God had given the same scripture, earlier. Then two days later, on April 27, 2014, Bishop James "Butch" Davis became a great source of encouragement. It was precisely what I needed. I felt like success was in my path. I needed to stay focused and stay on track. "Don't be side tracked!" is how I encouraged myself.

Two of my loyal supporters and good friends, lived in Atlanta. During my campaign, I visited their home and spent over two hours of precious time and received profound encouragement to propel me to the next level of endurance on this journey. On May 21, 2014, the District's other candidate and I arrived at the Virginia Annual Conference. We each spoke as candidates. It was a good test, like Abraham and Isaac on Mount Moriah. What I came to appreciate all the more is when you can't trust the process, or do not understand it, we must trust the promises of God. I reminded myself that, "He who promised is faithful."

These were challenging times on my journey. I also knew that *"God is no respecter of persons." and "All things work together for good to them that love God, to those who are the called according to His purpose."* I was reminded of the words of Hebrews 10:19 – 25: *"Let us hold fast the confession of hope without wavering, for he who has promised is faithful.*" Hallelujah!

God's grace was truly sufficient. I experienced His goodness in a wonderful way. At the Bishop's Council on June 23, 2014, the number of people who knew me and promised their support was a delightful creation of excitement, consolation, and confirmation. I prayed earnestly in my hour of success and triumph. "God, Jesus, Holy Spirit, I trust you! I cannot do this without you. I need your help, your power, your encouragement, your hope, and your protection. I need Godly wisdom to move in the right way. Please hear my cry, In Jesus's Name."

In the midst of the campaign, as I continued to pray and trust God, other life events continued to happen, to include the death of my father-in-law. He was funeralized on July 12, 2014, and I preached the funeral. After his burial, I flew back to Maryland for Sunday activities. With all going on in the world, family, and campaigning, traveling, speaking, and preaching, I was still pastor of Union Bethel AME Church. Thus, still in the midst of all my duties and responsibilities and life happenings, praying to my Heavenly Father was like breathing.

Then came July 2014. My reality was that the 50th Session of the AME General Conference was only two years away. I kept hearing in my spirit, the word, "More!" At this point in the campaign, I did not take anyone or anything, for granted. No opportunities were passed off as insignificant. When I was asked, "How is the campaign coming?" I answered, "I am encouraged by the people-at-large and my group." The General Board meeting was also encouraging. The group met and reaffirmed their support. I refused to be side-tracked. I was determined to focus on God and His promises, not the process. I needed more funds for campaigning. God was providing.

The other candidate's father and grandfather had become bishops in the AME Church, and the name and fame recognition could not be denied. The facts should not be undermined. And still I believed God was saying, "More! Keep your eyes on me" (just as he told Joshua and Caleb). "Don't follow the thoughts of the ten spies."

CHAPTER TEN

CHOSEN, but MUST CONTINUE TO RUN

In July 2016, at the 50th General Conference of the AME Church six bishops were elected. All six had experiences that led to that day of victory. My story is only one of them.

I had pastored Union Bethel AME Church for over a quarter of a century, (30 Years). God had given me great success and an increase in people and ministries, including inside and outside of the church. God even allowed me to be successful in the business world. This meant additional responsibilities and revenues. God was faithful to me.

In Matthew 6:19 – 33 God's word declares the following:

Lay not up for yourselves treasures upon earth, where moth and rust doth corrupt, and where thieves break through and steal: But lay up for yourselves treasures in heaven, where neither moth nor rust doth corrupt, and where thieves do not break through nor steal: For where your treasure is, there will your heart be also. The light of the body is the eye: if therefore thine eye be single, thy whole body shall be full of light. But if thine eye be evil, thy whole body shall be full of darkness. If therefore the light that is in thee be darkness, how great is that darkness! No man can serve two masters: for either he will hate the one and love the other; or else he will hold to the one and despise the other. Ye cannot serve God and mammon. Therefore, I say unto you, take no thought for your life, what ye shall eat, or what ye shall drink; nor yet for your body, what ye shall put on. Is not the life more than meat, and the body than raiment? Behold the fowls of the air: for they sow not, neither do they reap, nor gather into barns; yet your heavenly Father feedeth them. Are ye not much better than they? Which of you by taking thought can add one cubit unto his stature? And why take ye thought for raiment? Consider the lilies of the field, how they grow; they toil not, neither do they spin: And yet I say unto you, that even Solomon in all his glory was not arrayed like one of these. Wherefore, if God so clothes the grass of the field, which today is, and tomorrow is cast into the oven, shall HE not much more clothe you, O ye of little faith? Therefore, take no thought, saying, What shall we eat? or, What shall we drink? or, Wherewithal shall we be clothed? For after all these things do the Gentiles seek; for your heavenly Father knoweth that ye have need of all these things. But seek ye first the kingdom of God, and his righteousness, and all these things shall be added unto you."

I was now in the bishop race again, the third time. I was in the Word and the Word was in me.

"For the word is quick and powerful, and sharper than any two-edged sword, piercing even the dividing asunder of soul and spirit, and the joints and marrow, and is a discerner of the thoughts and intents of the heart," (Hebrews 4:12).

God was transforming me by the renewing of my mind. I was the patient in need. God was the doctor.

In the passage of Matthew 6:19–33, it is clear that Jesus was concerned about my heart and thoughts. Seven times He mentioned heart and/or thoughts in 16 verses. This certainly got my attention. I knew my heart and my motive had to be right with God. Purity and holiness are big qualities with God.

Many were praying for me! However, the most important ones praying on my behalf was the Holy Spirit and Jesus.

"Likewise, the Spirit also helps our infirmities: for we know not what we should pray as we ought, but the Spirit HIMSELF, makes intercession for us with groanings which cannot be uttered. And HE that searches the heart knows the mind of the Spirit because HE makes intercession for the saints according to the will of God,"

(Romans 8:27)

"Seeing then that we have a great high priest in the heavens, JESUS, the Son of God, let us hold fast to our profession. For we have not a high priest, which cannot be touched with the feeling of our infirmities, but was in all points tempted like as we are, yet without sin. Let us therefore come boldly unto the throne of grace, that we may obtain mercy and find grace to help in time of need,"

(Hebrews 4:12)

This was truly a time of need in my life. I needed HELP. I cried out to my God for HELP. I Honestly Entreated Love's Power: H.E.L.P. God heard my call and cry. He comforted me, confirmed me, and commanded me to go forward. I had every reason to believe in God. I was truly motivated to THINK BIG because God chose me, regardless of what others thought or said. I was determined to stay focused and finish strong.

I was ready to go now. The campaign trail would not be easy. But my heart, soul, mind, and body were clean through Jesus's Word as stated in John 15:3. And furthermore, in verses 15 and 16 Jesus says,

"Hence, I call you not servants; for the servant knows not what his Lord does; but I have called you friends; for all things that I have heard of my Father I have made known to you. You have not chosen ME, but I have chosen you, and ordained you, that you should go and bring forth fruit and that your fruit should remain that whatsoever you shall ask of the Father in my name, HE may give it to you."

CHAPTER ELEVEN

CHOSEN, but MUST FINISH STRONG

(Part I)

Two years of campaigning was all that was left at this point. Two years of uncertainty, still ahead. Two years of multi-tasking. I reminded myself that this is a process I must go through. There are no shortcuts and definitely no room for excuses!

It was July 15, 2014, at the Youth Congress Leadership Meeting when I felt so inadequate and so out of place. I had to be honest, now: *"Lord, please help me! I know I am untrusting yet trusting you. Thanks for my hope, which is in you. Please encourage my soul. I am tired. The night is long."*

The constant traveling was a necessity, but it was also challenging. The next day, I attended Bishop Vinton R. Anderson's funeral; who served as the 92nd Bishop of the AME Church. July 17th marked eight years to the day when I stood in Hampton, Virginia for the first time to announce my candidacy to become a bishop. I was reminded of the word: *"In all of your ways, acknowledge God, and He will direct your path,"* (Proverbs 3:6). Great is your faithfulness to me, O Lord!

I was truly being empowered by the Word of God. The *One Year Bible* reading for July 17th hit the nail on the head in Jeremiah 17:5 – 11, especially verse 5: *"Blessed is the man who trusts in the Lord and not in man."* Then Romans 4:16–25 put emphasis on exactly what I needed to be reminded of and to remember: *"He who promised is able to bring it to pass."*

Yes, beloveds! God is faithful to those who believe. My constant communion and conversation with my Heavenly Father were sustaining me. *"God, my fears are relieved when I think of your promises. As I am flying back from Bishop Anderson's funeral my heart is filled with thanksgiving. You have already done so much for me."*

On July 18, 2014, I got back on track. When I arrived home, I received a phone call to attend a meeting. The caller wanted to talk to me about something he heard that disturbed him. "Lord, help me!"

After this phone call and subsequent meeting, I began to travel a lot. My destinations included attendance at the Northwest Alabama Conference, in Birmingham; the Pittsburgh Conference; and then, back to Alabama to preach at the Southwest Alabama Conference. And I ended the month preaching at the 13th Episcopal District. These words resonated: *"You did not choose me, but I chose you to go forth and bear fruit,"* (John 15:16). This kept me going strong.

After a conversation with a prominent minister in the Washington Annual Conference of the 2nd Episcopal District and my Presiding Elder, I was feeling a little down. I prayed, *"God help me not to waver or doubt You. Help me! Encourage me!"* With that, I took off to campaign in Tyler, Texas, the 10th Episcopal District.

In October of 2014, I shifted gears. I felt a burst of fresh air. What a blessed, and encouraging time in Los Angeles, California. I felt more confident and less nervous in my presentations. There was excitement in the air! I started fasting from sweets. The results, spiritually and physically, were quite beneficial and pleasing. But I still had another trip to Alabama. This time I went to Mobile and Atmore.

I started running into a problem of people not following through on what they said or promised. Being rejected had now become my reality; however, I knew this was an integral part of the process. It was also a valuable step in reaching success. I resolved, *"I will trust God no matter what He allows to happen to me. God was and is in full control, directing my every step. Father, may I never allow man's rejection of me to be twisted with Your love to me and for me. Thanks for all You do to make my life worth living. In the name of Jesus, I pray. Amen!"*

On November 13, 2014, I preached at the Ebenezer AME Church's Men's Retreat in Ft. Washington, Maryland. What a blessing! This was truly a strong wind of support. They raised a little over $2,000 for my campaign. I continued to thank God for safe travels, protection, and love. I thanked Him for the support of family and friends. I thanked Him, also, for wisdom, provisions, and miracles.

When I attended the Rev. Winston Jones's (a son in ministry) retirement in South Carolina, I was fortunate to be able to visit the 7th District Planning Meeting. The 2014 Thanksgiving season brought me a wonderful experience of grace and favor through my son in the ministry, Pastor Sydney Williams, at Bethel AME Church in Morristown, New Jersey.

I then journeyed to Nashville, Tennessee on November 19, 2014. I was thinking so heavily of my mother who had passed away on this day nine years earlier. *"God, you have been so faithful, kind, and true. Please touch me, help me, and encourage me. Grant me success, in Jesus' name."*

As this calendar year was drawing to a close, I felt a tremendous need for God. I mused over it. I expressed myself to God with openness. I wanted God's blessing, and I wanted to be a blessing. Two thousand fifteen was almost here and the time left for campaigning was only 18 months.

I needed support from Africa. So, I flew to Cape Town, South Africa. While there, I heard that someone whom I thought would support me actually was not supporting me.

When May 15, 2015 arrived, my support was strong. I visited the Atlanta North Annual Conference in the AME 6th Episcopal District. I was welcomed at the Baltimore, Washington, and Virginia Annual Conferences. I was elected as the lead delegate in the Washington Conference. I received a wonderful endorsement from Bishop Phillip Cousin, Jr., the 96th AME Bishop. I was encouraged by the outpouring of support from so many people. The prayers, donations, words, and love were outstanding.

The Spirit of God led me to Psalm 37. Jesus, my intercessor, was praying for me and I appreciated that so much. I was feeling victory in the atmosphere. I proceeded to touch every possible base by making trips to the North Carolina Annual Conference and an Annual Conference in Dayton, Ohio.

While all this was happening on the road, real fires, many challenging fires, were burning at Union Bethel. At first there was just a few, but as time moved on, many fires broke out. I needed strength, Godly wisdom, supernatural spiritual power for discernment, and right decision-making. *"Father please, keep me encouraged. I need help."*

The issues were plentiful! Music/sound, Bethel House/ Outreach, sewage installation project, SFB concerns, sick and shut-in members, usher ministry issues, and ongoing financial challenges. I cried out! *"Have mercy and help me, Lord!"* We prayed and prayed and kept on praying.

I sought after the Lord for the forgiveness of my sins by thoughts, words, and deeds. I pleaded with God to hear my call for H.E.L.P. I admitted that I was weak and inadequate. The fears and the politics were real. I was tired! I needed rest. I needed to be recharged. I cried out! *"God help me to rest in you!"* At this point, I had an entire year left of campaigning.

On June 3, 2015, in Wilmington and Durham, North Carolina, God showed His faithfulness one more time. This time, the encouragement came through a call and a conversation of over 30 minutes. Shortly thereafter, I received another sizable financial donation. Praise The Lord!

I cried out to God for help, to relax in His love, power, and provisions. There were concerns about deceptions and lies spreading throughout the campaign process; however, Isaiah 54:17 gave me the blessed assurance that

> *"No weapon that is formed against you shall prosper, and every tongue that shall rise against you in the judgment YOU shall condemn."*

I took a deep breath, dug my heels in and stared at the final year of campaigning before the July 2016 election for bishop. This was a new season in my life. For me there was no looking back, no regrets, no holding back, no turning back. My ever-refreshing word came from Psalm 27.

In June 2015, Union Bethel hosted a great pastoral anniversary celebration for my family and me. And just as quickly as the celebrations ended, tragedy struck in Charleston, South Carolina at Mother Emanuel AME Church. I attended the now late Pastor Clemente Pinckney's funeral. As you know, President Barack Obama spoke. I grieved with the families. I was so pleased, proud, and privileged to be connected with the African Methodist Episcopal Church. I had a new appreciation for my church's display of love, discipline, and forgiveness as Jesus the Christ did on the cross of crucifixion.

My prayers were now immersed in the Spirit of God to know the right places to travel. I knew I could not go or be everywhere. At the same time, I realized I needed to be where I needed to be. I was called to the bedside of a bishop who had been given a fatal diagnosis, to offer prayer and comfort to the family. Afterwards, my son and grandson, Matthew and Cameron, and I attended the AME General Board meeting in New Orleans.

Unfortunately, I could not be at Union Bethel as much now. My life had now become more than an adventure, it was a FAITH ADVENTURE. It was a **F**ANTASTIC **A**DVENTURE **I**N **T**RUSTING **H**IM. Although South Carolina is my home state, I was born, raised, and went to undergraduate school there, I did not take my home state for granted. I visited and campaigned in Charleston, Sumter, and Florence. I attended the Seventh District's Education Conference, and annual conferences, young adult luncheon, and lay biennial. With all of that, the joy of my labor came to me when Pastor Nate Thomas, a Baptist pastor in

Maryland, called me. He said, *"I dreamed that you were elected on the first ballot."* I responded in prayer. *"Lord, do it for me!"*

This was truly a time of uncertainty. I had to take one day at a time. I had to wait on God. I had to trust God despite all outward appearances.

CHAPTER TWELVE

CHOSEN, but MUST FINISH STRONG

(Part II)

At this point, only nine months remained in the campaign. I likened it to how women must feel when carrying a baby. Every day was a new day. I had to start each day with the right attitude, right behavior, right commitment, determination, energy, faith, and hard work. There was no room for pity parties. If I wanted to be reborn as a bishop, I had to carry this dream all the way to the day of its birth.

The last three months of 2015, were challenging, refreshing, and fruitful. I started it out with an unexpected Presidential Suite in the Holiday Inn arranged by a dear friend who knew the owner as well as my need for rest and renewal. This empowered me to get moving to finish 2015 strong, zig-zagging the country and touching every necessary base in the process.

During those three months, I made more than 30 stops and visits to multiple key states, cities, and conferences. The cities included Pine Bluff and Little Rock, Arkansas; Charleston, South Carolina; Chicago, Illinois; Phoenix City, Alabama; Durham, North Carolina; Jacksonville, Florida; Philadelphia, Pennsylvania; and then, back to Charleston. It was in Charleston when God showed me rainbows in the sky. What could I do, but testify? *"What a mighty God we serve. Angels bow before Him. Heaven and earth adore Him."*

Despite the tedious travel schedule, I experienced the continual presence of God. His mercy and His grace led me and surrounded me with inspiration and strong confirmation that God, and only God, could make things work out. I did a workshop on deliverance from debt at the Second Episcopal District's Deliverance Conference. I preached at many of the annual conferences, mid-year conferences, gave remarks at others, and was recognized at all of them. Everything was going well. To add joy to the journey, campaign finances were flowing in the right direction. At least three deaths of close family members and friends occurred that got me off track, but I was able to reset and refocus. Thanksgiving Day was an incredible time and gave me a new appreciation for my nuclear family and the place I called home.

The great ecstasy of November 2015 was followed by a disturbing dream in December. I woke up on December 3rd from a dream that implied that I was not elected in 2016 because of 135 votes that were disqualified. I became fearful. While looking out the window from my bedroom altar, I saw two bright stars shining in the sky; they reminded me of Abraham. He hoped against hope. He did not waver, but against all odds he believed God.

Of course, this was a time of severe testing for me. I sometimes lacked the courage to stand as a man of God in certain private situations. However, I confessed my weaknesses, and my fears to God. I cried out to Him who was able. "Please, help me, this day, in Jesus' name. Help me Lord!" Integrity, truth, and protection are what I needed that morning.

The HELP call was desperation! I needed it and wanted it. I **H**onestly **E**ntreated the **L**ord's **P**ower! It works and it works. I had to persist in dealing with reading God's Word, the promises, the blessings, the serving, praising, and worshipping, and taking it one day at a time.

I came to my right mind. I woke up from the temporary stupor of the fear of evil. I remembered that, *"The Lord is my Shepherd, and I will fear no evil."* I said! *"Please Lord, forgive me, love me, help me, encourage me, and bring me out. Thanks for Your mercy, grace, power, peace, and love."* This experience was at an excellent time. It prepared me to fly to Charleston to attend the Congress of National Black Churches (CNBC) Conference at Mother Emanuel AME Church on the same airplane with other candidates.

The day after Christmas 2015, my family and I went to Punta Cana, Dominican Republic. This family vacation was much needed. God had done miracles for all of us, and we were grateful. The rainbow appeared again. It was now December 27, 2015.

January 2016 was equivalent to the last quarter of a football game. This is it! From now on I needed to visit an average of three cities per week. Yet, I had to stay healthy. This was a tremendous challenge. I was not exercising adequately because of the schedule and circumstances. I had to fulfill my Connectional Church responsibilities. I was still the treasurer of the 2nd Episcopal District, serving on the Red Board as treasurer (the 2nd District's non-profit) and as an executive in the Washington Annual Conference. My wife really stepped up during this time. During the last 6 months of the campaign, she took over coordinating Union Bethel's 2nd worship site.

So much had been accomplished in 30 years. To sharpen my skills, I completed a leadership coaching series from Dr. Mickey

Burmin and attended the AME Evangelism Conference in Memphis. I preached at various places plus made it to the CNBC gathering at Mother Emanuel in Charleston. Then I couldn't miss the Turner Theological Seminary Founder's Day in Atlanta, nor the AME Women's Missionary Society (WMS) Executive Board Meeting in Greensboro, North Carolina. But in the midst of all this, Union Bethel was doing much better spiritually, numerically, and financially. Five years earlier, I started a morning telephone prayer line where Union Bethel members and friends prayed daily (except Sundays). In 2016, with joy and glory to God, we celebrated the fifth year of this time of prayer that helped transform the church in many ways. Amid this, Sherita and I celebrated 34 years of marriage.

There were so many business meetings. The future of WE KLEEN, and other things such as my 60th birthday celebration and the 30th year celebration of pastoring Union Bethel were critical. The main thing, however, that would properly culminate the long three-year journey was only one thing: winning in Philadelphia. Being elected in July 2016 was the goal.

On April 13, 2016, I started praying for my fellow candidates, *"Lord please give us all success today. Give us all the victory. Bless mightily! Continue to give grace, mercy, and favor to us all in the name of Jesus."*

Those last thirty days prior to the opening of the General Conference in July 2016 were still days of uncertainty, intensity, and complexity. Yet, God was involved and in charge. The humanity's free will had its place. It was clear that people had a plan, but God had another. A better way of saying it, perhaps, is that God had a plan, and people could not alter, prevent, or pervert that plan.

There was much talk about six openings to be filled by newly-elected bishops. Everyone seemed to be on one accord with that number. However, who these six people would or should be, varied greatly through the AME leaders and the conference delegates. I learned that my name finally got mentioned as a sure victor for one of the openings. The word was out that I most probably would be elected on the fifth or sixth ballot. Some thought that my own words, "God had chosen me," may come back to hurt me.

Sooner or later, a person must learn to let go completely, 100%, and let God take the reins or the steering wheel. We did! I did! I celebrated. I received encouragement from the same prayer line that God used me to encourage others. Union Bethel Church needed a financial miracle. "But God." I prayed, "Please help them!" Then, I took a trip to Jamaica, sunny Jamaica. I thanked God immensely for that period of rest and relaxation. I could not thank God enough.

The rest and restoration helped me tremendously to finish strong during the time of the General Conference. I missed a lot by taking this campaign journey. However, after all that I had missed in the past three years, I thank God that I did not miss what happened on July 11, 2016, in Philadelphia, Pennsylvania. At the 50th Session of the General Conference of the African Methodist Episcopal Church, I was elected a bishop on the first ballot.

The political talk had been interesting. As I mentioned earlier word by the church experts was that I would become a bishop but not until the fifth or sixth ballot. One person even stood up with a strong suggestion and interesting persuasion on behalf of a particular candidate being selected first. He recommended that all other candidates back down, so only one person be considered or elected first. But God had not spoken yet. The people had not spoken to confirm the will and word of God.

To my utter surprise and everyone else's surprise also, the first name that showed up after the first ballot was mine! In order to be elected a bishop, I needed 741 votes: I received 941. For a moment,

I was speechless. I was caught off guard. Then I remembered the word of the Lord. *"Is there anything too hard for God? The things which are impossible to man is possible with God,"* (Jeremiah 32:27; Matthew 19:26)?

I shouted to the top of my voice! *"That's me! I won! I have been elected. I won on the first ballot! It was prophesied in the dream. It's true. Praise The Lord! Thank you, Father! Praise The Lord! Thank you, Holy Spirit. Thank you, Sherita. Thank you, family. Thank you, people and prayer partners. To God be the glory!"*

I am so thankful to be the 133rd elected and consecrated bishop in the 200-year-old AME Church. Being elected first and on the first ballot election made the victory even more special, spectacular, and mind-boggling. What a humbling moment! God had given me another chance to serve more, farther, wider, deeper, and higher.

The purple robe, the consecration and ordination that once was a mystery is now history. The purple robe is my reality. To God be the glory. You did choose me! I am and will be eternally thankful.

Hush! Hush! Harry L. Seawright, somebody's calling your name and saying, *"Can't you see, Harry L. Seawright, nothing is too hard for me! A thousand years is as a day for me. Now go! Tell others that I have a plan for them too. I am God! There is none like me. There is no respecter of persons, with me. What I have done in principle for Harry L. Seawright and others, I will do for you.*

LIFE AFTER DEATH

When I died, and God brought me back to life, everything changed: nothing remained the same.

I live every moment as if the next second may not happen. Every thought is about "What if?". Every moment is another chance to live life with purpose and do all I can to make life count. Life's existence becomes a moment of gratitude. Every blessing is a miracle. I realize that I am living on borrowed time. I see every moment as another chance to get it right with God, family, friends, ministry, and my life's assignments.

How can I make the most of this valuable opportunity? Seeking forgiveness, praying for strength and improvement. I constantly ask, "Have I done all I can? Did I give it my best? Did I treat everyone I right? Did I do right by God and my people, family and friends? Did I show appreciation for the many things that went right?"

Friday, October 28, 2016, is forever etched in my mind. That was the day I died, but also the day God brought me back to life. This day was the birthday of a new adventure, a rebirth, a re-engagement of my life and purpose. My "Good Friday", the day I wrestled with an angel and got my limp, my Damascus Road experience. As of this writing all of that happened nine years ago. I honestly can say that seemed like the worst day of my life; however, it worked out to be a pivotal day for me to start living my best life. God has been and continues to rewrite my life. He has given me a new perspective and outlook. He as rebranded me, as well as recycled me. I *feel* life, whole and filled with purpose and peace.

Let me explain. Like a butterfly, I went through a metamorphic stage. Like a baby struggling to be born from the womb. Like a clay jar being broken and remade by the potter (Jeremiah 18); like the Apostle Paul and others being renewed, God has done all of that for me. I often think about Lazarus being called from death to life (St. John 11). How might he describe experiencing new life? I think about the 12-year-old girl (St. Mark 12), the widow's son for whom Jesus stopped the funeral procession, told the young man to get up and live, then gave him to his weeping mother (St. Luke 8). What about the countless others, like Dorcas the seller of purple linen, the young man who fell out of the window to his death?

There is not much written about the testimony of the above list of people and countless others, but I want to share my testimony. I pray that others will be blessed and know that God is able (Ephesians 3:20-21). God give miracles to those who He knows will give Him all honor and glory. I live to give my testimony. On October 31, 2016, the morning of my quadruple by-pass surgery, I promised God that if He would bring me through this medical ordeal, I would testify at every door He opened for me.

October 28, 2016, started out as a trip to New York. My goal was to visit Dr. Melvin Greene, a good friend and brother whose wife suffered a brain aneurysm a few months earlier. Doctors gave her a slim chance of surviving. I booked a flight to New York City to visit them at their home. During our sophomore year at Benedict College, Melvin was my roommate. Almost 50 years later our friendship continues. We are fraternity brothers. He is my tax accountant and advisor for many of my business and ministry decision. We were together a few months earlier as he and his wife Bettye joined me in Philadelphia, Pennsylvania, encouraging me in my election as a Bishop. His nephew Rev.

Dr. Travis Greene, the renowned preacher and recording artist, rendered a concert at a local church as a fund raiser in support of my campaign to be elected.

I awoke that Friday around 4:00 am to board a 6:00 am flight to New York. My schedule included a change of flights in Detroit, Michigan. I was due to land in New York's John F. Kennedy Airport at approximately 11:00 am. I woke up that morning, did my daily devotions, prayers, read *The One Year Bible* daily reading, showered, dressed and gathered my bags that I packed the night before. I boarded the flight and landed in Detroit. The new gate in the airport was extremely far from my arrival gate. Being unfamiliar with the airport, I did not see signs for the tram that carried passengers between concourses. Therefore, I walked the entire distance.

When I arrived at my departure gate, I was anxious and tired. I preceded to the restroom and heard the announcement for my time to board. Since First Class passengers boarded first, I appreciated being able to rest a moment and catch my breath. Suddenly, I felt a horrible pain over my entire body. I asked myself, "My God, what is this?".

The next thing I remembered was waking up in an ambulance. The paramedic asked me if I knew what happened to me. When I said I didn't know, he said, "You collapsed in the airport. We did everything we could to revive you and after 2 failed CPR attempts and a shock with a defibrillator, you were pronounced dead. I decided to massage your chest and you just woke up!" At that point he and his assistant put me on oxygen and preceded to cut off my clothes. We were headed to a small nearby hospital to confirm my death.

When I arrived at the hospital, I asked for my cell phone. I wanted to call Sherita, my wife and inform her of what was going on. When I reached her I explained that I had gone into cardiac arrest, been declared dead, but my heart was beating again. I told her, "I am alive and I wanted to tell you myself". I couldn't talk to her long, but I let her know that after doctors examined me, they decided to transfer me to a hospital in Detroit that was known for excellent cardiac care. I told Sherita I was ok and would keep her posted. After a thorough examination it was discovered that I had four blockages in my heart's arteries and needed a quadruple heart bypass.

First, I thanked God for sparing my life. Then I made a promise to God that I trusted His will for my life. I promised Him that I accepted and believed in His prefect plan for my life, as well for as my family and future. Sherita came to Detroit first; Shari and Cameron arrived later that evening. Matthew rode with friends and arrived during the weekend. Following a suggestion from Matthew, I made a live video of my personal update and a plea for prayer. As a result of Matthew posting the video on Facebook, what seemed like thousands of prayers, many visits followed. Early my Monday morning, October 31st, I was ushered into surgery. I was operated on by a Christian surgeon by the name of Dr. Tim Sell who had a prayer with me and I had the best medical team and staff at Belmont Hospital. My recuperation was speedy. The second day, tubes were removed, and I was up walking the hallway. Dr. Sell did an unusual procedure that gave several promises for a longer life.

The biggest complication I faced after was the damage caused by the tubes that were down my throat during surgery to my vocal cords. I remained hoarse for several months. I faced fluid buildup two months later, but after cardio rehab that issue was resolved. My testimony is that what I thought was one of the worst days of my life has now become the best day that has reshaped and renewed my life and zest for life and living in such a manner I am now living my best life.

MEET BISHOP SEAWRIGHT

Bishop Harry L. Seawright serves as the 133rd elected and consecrated Bishop of the African Methodist Episcopal (AME) Church. His election marked a historic moment during the church's 50th Quadrennial General Conference as he became only the second bishop to be elected on the first ballot.

On December 12, 2025, he was appointed by the Council of Bishops to the Second Episcopal District to serve as the Presiding Prelate over five Annual Conferences: Baltimore, Washington, Virginia, North Carolina, and Western North Carolina. He also serves as Chair of the AME Commission on Christian Education. From 2019 to 2020, he faithfully led the denomination as President of the Council of Bishops.

From 2016 to 2024, Bishop Seawright served as Presiding Prelate of the Ninth Episcopal District, (the State of Alabama). On August 28, 2024, during the 52nd Quadrennial Session of the African Methodist Episcopal Church in Columbus, Ohio, he received his Episcopal assignment as Presiding Prelate of the Thirteenth Episcopal District (the Commonwealth of Kentucky and the State of Tennessee).

Born in Swansea, South Carolina, Bishop Seawright is the youngest child of the late Joe Nathan and Mary L. Seawright. A fourth-generation AME, his faith was deeply nurtured at Prodigal AME Church in Swansea, South Carolina. His humble beginnings and spiritual foundation continue to illuminate and sustain his lifelong commitment to faith and service.

Bishop Seawright earned a Bachelor of Science degree in Business Administration from Benedict College in Columbia,

South Carolina. He received the Master of Divinity degree from Howard University School of Divinity in Washington, D.C. where he was honored with the award for "Student Most Likely to Excel in Pastoral Ministry." He earned the Doctor of Ministry degree from Howard University and was named "Doctor of Ministry Student of the Year" for his exceptional doctoral project. He has received numerous additional honors including participating in the University of Oxford Roundtable in Oxford, England.

Throughout his ministerial journey, Bishop Seawright was admitted to the Central Annual Conference of the Seventh Episcopal District by the late Bishop Frank Madison Reid, II and appointed to serve as Interim Pastor of St. Stephen AME Church in St. Matthews, South Carolina. He was ordained an Itinerant Deacon by the late Bishop Henry Wendell Murph and an Itinerant Elder by the late Bishop John Hurst Adams. Over a distinguished pastoral career spanning 35 years, he served congregations at Payne Memorial AME Church in Jessup, Maryland; Hemingway Temple AME Church in Washington, D.C.; and Union Bethel AME Church in Brandywine and Temple Hills, Maryland.

Bishop Seawright is the author of *More Than Bricks and Mortar: Building a Church Without Losing Your Mind* and *Don't Faint: Help for Hurting Pastors and Their Families*. His practical and transparent writings continue to encourage, guide, and strengthen pastors, leaders, and congregations.

In addition to his pastoral and Episcopal leadership, Bishop Seawright has served the church and broader community in numerous capacities, including the AME International Commission on Economic Development, the AME International Health Commission, Second Vice President of the Trustee Board at Turner Theological Seminary at the Interdenominational

Theological Center, the Church Mutual Insurance African American Leaders Advisory Committee, and the AstraZeneca U.S. Health Equity Advisory Council. In 2018, he was inducted into Sigma Pi Phi Fraternity.

As an entrepreneur, Bishop Seawright is the founder and co-owner of WeKleen, Inc., HLS Consulting, Trinity Group, and Prestigious Property Management. He continues to apply his business expertise to advance community development and promote positive societal change.

Bishop Seawright is married to the former Sherita Gayle Moon. They are the proud parents of Ms. Shari Nicole and the Reverend Harry Matthew Seawright, and the loving grandparents of Minister Cameron Isaiah Seawright.

www.ingramcontent.com/pod-product-compliance
Lightning Source LLC
Chambersburg PA
CBHW030029280726
48869CB00043B/1046
* 9 7 8 1 9 6 8 4 4 2 1 0 1 *